WEAVING
on a
LITTLE
LOOM
Date: 12/17/18

WEAVING on a LITTLE LOOM

TECHNIQUES, PATTERNS, AND PROJECTS FOR BEGINNERS

FIONA DALY

PRINCETON ARCHITECTURAL PRESS · NEW YORK

Published by
Princeton Architectural Press
A McEvoy Group company
202 Warren Street
Hudson, New York 12534
www.papress.com

Printed and bound in China
21 20 19 18 4 3 2 1 First edition

ISBN: 978-1-61689-712-3

Conceived, edited, and designed by
Quarto Publishing plc
an imprint of The Quarto Group
6 Blundell Street
London N7 9BH
www.quartoknows.com

QUAR.LOOM

Text and pattern/project designs: Fiona Daly
Editor: Kate Burkett
Senior art editor: Jackie Palmer
Designer: Grand Union Design
Photographers: Nicki Dowey, Phil Wilkins, and Mary Daly
(page 9)
Illustrator: Kuo Kang Chen
Art director: Caroline Guest
Creative director: Moira Clinch
Publisher: Samantha Warrington

Library of Congress Cataloging-in-Publication Data is
available from the publisher upon request.

Printed in China

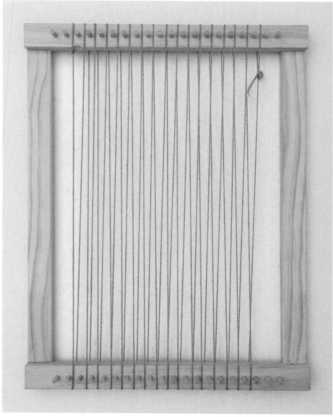

CONTENTS

———

———

MEET FIONA

———

Hello! My name is Fiona Daly and I'm a textile designer-maker, and weaver. Currently based in a humble studio in South London, I specialize in creating a range of soft furnishings and accessories made with natural British wools in my bespoke woven designs. I sell my work through contemporary craft fairs and my online shop, selling a variety of products—from cushions to throws to lampshades and shawls. I also run a program of weaving workshops on frame and table looms from my studio and at various pop-up locations.

———

My love of constructed textiles began at an early age, influenced by my grandmother, who worked as a lacemaker and ran her own craft shop in the West of Ireland. It was a natural progression that I went on to study Textile Design at the National College of Art and Design, Ireland. During these highly creative stimulating years, I also had the opportunity to study in Bergen, Norway, where my appreciation of traditional crafts and natural materials grew. After graduating, I honed my weaving skills while working for a handweaver in the West of Ireland.

Since then, my weaving journey has evolved many strands. Through being awarded a residency in a weaving center in the Shetland Islands, I greatly developed my woven design skills and I was introduced to the most amazing material, Shetland wool. During my years in Edinburgh, I was involved in a multi-disciplinary craft workshop, where I began teaching weaving courses and fell in love with it! It was also here that I had the wholly enriching experience of working in the weaving workshop of a Rudolf Steiner-inspired organization. During this time I came to acquire the most beautiful weaving loom—a George Wood dobby loom, a traditional, manual loom with highly complex capabilities where the pattern can be manually programmed by hammering tiny wooden pegs into holes on lags and chains. This has allowed me to push my design skills further and stretch my technical knowledge of weave. Throughout all of this, my love of natural materials, in particular of wool and of particular sheep breeds, continues to grow, along with my interest in sustainable, environmentally friendly textiles.

While weaving can be inherently complex and technical, it provides a fantastic framework for creative expression. One of the reasons I love weaving so much is that it engages both the left and the right sides of the brain. As weaving has developed over thousands of years, one could spend a lifetime studying it and still there would be more to learn. Yet, it can be paired back to a basic principle. Weaving is not a process to be mastered overnight; it requires a lot of patience and practice to understand its magnificent capabilities. The world of weaving is so diverse and complex, with such a variety of looms available, and with such an array of large, expensive equipment, it would be easy to be put off this craft. However, with its origins as a primitive craft, I have realized that it is possible to create beautiful, distinguished weaving with only the most basic of equipment and the most sparse of toolkits. This book aims to guide the novice weaver embarking on this exciting craft!

In this book, you will be introduced to the basics of frame loom weaving—the simplest of weaving looms and therefore, the perfect one to begin weaving with—through a series of technique tutorials, together with complete project guides. Do not be discouraged if, at first, your weaving is loose with gaping holes, lacks uniform edges, is squint, or if little skips appear in the pattern. Learn to love these imperfections that represent your weaving journey, and know that their decrease maps your progression as a budding weaver. It takes time to master the tension and beat of woven threads and experience to fully appreciate the handle of your chosen material. Relish in the knowledge that you are continuing a traditional craft that has been in continuous practice for almost 10,000 years and is intrinsic to the heritage of cultures the world over.

You will become a master of your own patience and notice how the process of weaving calms and slows things right down. You will tune everything else out and solely concentrate on counting numbers, over and under, while feeling the most beautiful of natural materials feed through your hands. Weaving by hand can be labor intensive and slow—a true slow textile—but the rewards are unrivaled. Not only will you come away with a handcrafted woven product, but you will have the satisfaction of the enjoyment gained from the time spent in the making process—it is quite the rewarding accomplishment!

CHAPTER 1

WELCOME TO WEAVING

THE HISTORY OF WEAVING

—

Weaving is a form of constructed textile. Most people are familiar with knitting, which consists of knotted loops made of one continuous strand and worked on two needles. The structure of weaving is different: weaving consists of two sets of interlacing components that are perpendicular to each other. In the weaving of textiles, these components are called threads.

—

The vertical set of threads that runs the length of the fabric is called the warp. The horizontal threads that run the width of the fabric are called the weft. In the simplest interlacement of these sets of threads, the weft weaves over the first warp thread and under the next, and so on to the end of the row or "pick." The next weft weaves under and over, and so on. Warp threads need to be held taut so that they can be woven in the most efficient way. This requires a structure or device—a loom. This is any type of device, regardless of how basic or complex it may be, that holds warp threads in tension. Weaving can range from being very simple to extremely complex in terms of the looms, yarns, and interlacement of the threads, to produce a range of patterns of increasing intricacy.

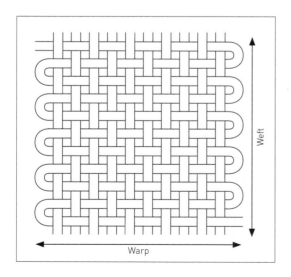

Warp and Weft: This diagram illustrates the simple interlacement of over-one, under-one of plain weave.

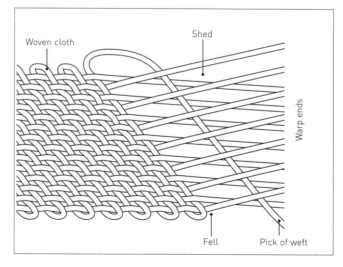

What is Weaving: This diagram illustrates the weaving process, showing warp, weft, shed, fell, pick, and woven cloth. All of these terms are explained in the glossary (pages 140–141).

Weaving cloth is the second oldest form of textile-making in the world. This machine room (top) in the Boott Cotton Mills Museum in Lowell, USA, is identical to the working conditions in the late 19th century.

Machine weaving is a complex process. This yarn warping machine (above) shows eight different-colored warp threads being woven at the same time.

Weaving cloth is the second oldest form of textile-making in the world, dating back almost 10,000 years. However, the process of weaving actually predates the weaving of threads to make cloth. In fact, mankind developed weaving while still wearing animal skins! Indeed, primitive weaving first developed through the weaving of natural, local, and available materials such as willow and reeds. These were woven in the round to make baskets. Basketry found in Guitarrero Cave, in Peru, dates from 8,000 BC.

Woven-cloth construction developed later, once yarn spinning had been invented. Yarns could be woven into cloths that were softer and finer than anything that had gone before. This created the need for a device that could tension one set of threads so that they could be woven with another. It is thought that civilization developed independently in six different parts of the world, and it is most probable that the loom evolved independently for different logistical reasons, too.

A history of weaving is not complete without mentioning Ancient Peru. The study of Peruvian textiles is fascinating for the modern-day weaver. Their skill in weaving is unparalleled and, over thousands of years, they have developed many techniques with amazing skill and creativity. It is no wonder that Peruvian textiles are a constant source of inspiration for weavers all over the world.

In more recent times, the British Industrial Revolution of the mid-18th century was sparked by advances in the textile industry, primarily the development of the weaving loom, the flying shuttle, spinning and carding machines, and, finally, the power loom. Such inventions changed weaving forever, as machines replaced the hand-weaving skills of workers in mills. In response, through the Arts and

Weaving is practiced worldwide. Ikat is woven (left) ready to sell in Indonesia and a Peruvian woman (above) weaves colorful alpaca wool.

Crafts Movement of the 19th century, William Morris sought to revive these hand skills and so prevent them dying out.

Perhaps this is somewhere near where we are today in the world of weaving. People are not weaving out of a necessity to make cloth, but rather as a choice; as a pastime and a return to the handmade, learning traditional skills in response to ongoing advancements in the technological world. There has certainly been a revival of craft in the past two decades or so, the indie-craft movement married with the designer-maker movement having created a positive shift in how craft is viewed and perceived.

I think it is fantastic that weaving—through the lap-loom weaving craze—is now "having a moment" and being introduced to so many new people throughout the world. Weaving is grounding and has been proven to have therapeutic benefits— engaging both the mind and hands, crossing over the core, and restoring balance. I think people are searching for this in the Digital Age.

This book is an attempt to place lap-loom weaving (which I hope will prove to be more than just a trend) in context within the world of weaving and to give the new weaver an understanding of traditional techniques, as well as an appreciation of where they originated, how they evolved, and the language associated with them. This book is a contemporary take on those traditional techniques and aims to teach you the skills you need to experiment further. The projects toward the back of the book are aimed at inspiring the lap-loom weaver to see beyond a woven wall hanging, for example, and to embrace the creativity and diversity that all kinds of weaving have to offer!

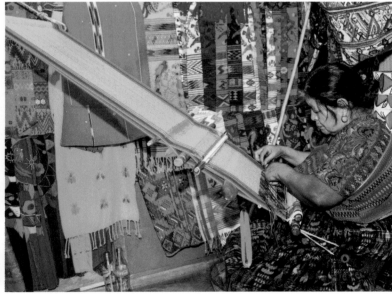

A Sask tribe woman weaves in Sade, Lombok, Indonesia (left) and a Mayan woman weaves with a strap loom in Antigua, Guatemala.

CHOOSING YOUR LOOM

———

A loom is any device on which threads can be held taut and therefore woven. Looms come in many different shapes and sizes, ranging from the most basic to the most complex. This book focuses on frame looms, or "lap looms" as they are becoming known, which are most closely related to tapestry looms. They are a simplified, smaller-scale version, making them the perfect loom with which to begin your weaving journey.

———

Frame looms are relatively cheap and accessible in comparison with their other loom cousins. They also come in various shapes and sizes. All operate according to the same principle, but some may be more suitable for particular projects. In this section, I examine three types of frame loom, including the ones used for the projects that feature later in the book, as well as provide instructions on how to make your own cardboard version.

When choosing a loom, things to bear in mind include its size, as well as the sett, yarn weight, and weaving style. You will also need to consider the weaving environment: Where will you be weaving and how much space do you have? How would you prefer to sit while you work—with the loom upright and clamped to a table, or on a smaller lap loom? What size is the project you wish to make? With frame looms, you can only weave to three-quarters of the frame size. How tightly spaced do the warp threads need to be for your weaving? Do you intend to weave a lot of warp-faced or evenly balanced weaves? Or will you focus on more weft-faced, tapestry weaving? Will you be creating a variety of weave structures or focusing mainly on plain weave?

My favorite of these looms is the frame loom studded with pegs across the top and bottom bar, because it is an excellent multipurpose loom. You can easily vary the sett, with limited movement of the warp threads with a higher e.p.i.

BASIC FRAME LOOM

This type of loom is the most basic, and is essentially a strong, rectangular frame. There is no guidance for warp spacing on this loom, but strips of masking tape dotted with measured increments across the frame bars can act as a guide. This makes it a very flexible loom in terms of sett. A basic frame loom is also suitable for double-sided weaving. This means that it is possible to weave a front and a back cloth seamlessly attached in a tubular structure, as in the project for the *Looped Bag* (see pages 130–139). An old picture frame can be used as a quick and improvized basic frame loom—just make sure that it is quite sturdy.

FRAME LOOM WITH PEGS

This type of loom is a slight development from the basic frame loom. It is designed so that warp threads can be wound around pegs (or nails, as used in some homemade versions) that run across the top and bottom bars, for a simple warping technique. It is also very effective with the figure-eight warping method (see page 36). Like the basic frame loom, it is quite easy to increase the sett on this loom, too.

FRAME WITH SLITS

This loom is very similar to the frame loom with pegs. However, instead of pegs, slits are used to hold the warp threads in place, according to a predetermined spacing. Adjusting the sett is not as straightforward with this type of loom.

Masking tape with measured increments

BASIC FRAME LOOM

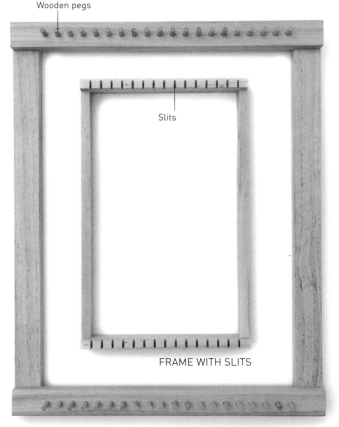

Wooden pegs

Slits

FRAME WITH SLITS

FRAME LOOM WITH PEGS

THE CARDBOARD LOOM

A cardboard loom is where it all began for me! This is an excellent loom to make at home, so I have included instructions on how to do so here. Some advantages of this loom are that it is not a big investment, money-wise; you can decide on an appropriate size, depending on the project; and it is also suitable for double-sided weaving. However, no natural shed can be formed and the sett cannot be altered, once this has been decided. A cardboard loom works best with a wide sett.

YOU WILL NEED

Strong, thick cardboard—
6 in. (15 cm) longer/taller
than desired size of finished
piece—at least 160 lb
(400 gsm)
Ruler
Pencil
Craft knife/paper scissors
2 x corrugated cardboard
strips, measuring the loom
width x 1 in. (2.5 cm) height
Glue

1–4

5

1 Lay the piece of cardboard on a flat surface and measure ⅝ in. (1.5 cm) from the top edge with the ruler. Draw a horizontal line across the top of the card, ⅝ in. (1.5 cm) from the edge of the cardboard, as measured. Measure a further ⅝ in. (1.5 cm) from this line and draw a second horizontal line.

2 Repeat Step 1 across the bottom edge of the piece of cardboard.

3 According to the sett required (i.e. how many warp threads you would like per inch/2.5 cm), mark the first horizontal line you drew in Step 1 at the top of the cardboard with measured increments. In this example, to keep things simple, I marked every ½ in. (1 cm), so that there will be one warp thread every ½ in. (1 cm). Also mark ½-in. (1-cm) increments along the top edge of the cardboard, in line with the marks along the first horizontal line.

4 Repeat the ½-in. (1-cm) marking across the first line you drew at the bottom of the cardboard and also along the bottom edge.

5 Using the scissors or craft knife, cut a slit from the first dot on the top edge of the cardboard to the corresponding dot marked on the first line. The slit will measure ⅝ in. (1.5 cm). Make sure to cut the line straight. Continue in this way until all the dots along the top of the cardboard have been joined by a cut slit. Repeat this process across the bottom of the cardboard.

6 Line up the two strips of corrugated cardboard with the second horizontal lines drawn in Step 1 and glue them in place. The strips of card make it easier to raise warp threads and provide a firm base to begin weaving on.

<u>6</u>

7 To dress the loom, tie the beginning of the warp yarn in an overhand knot (see *Knots*, page 97), leaving a ⅘ in (2cm) tail. Place the knot and tail into the first slit on the top left-hand side, so that the knot sits on the reverse side of the loom. Wind the warp under tension from the top to the bottom on the front side. Pass it through the first slit at the bottom, in line with the slit at the top. The active yarn is now on the reverse of the cardboard. Feed it through the next adjacent slit to the right. Wind the active yarn under tension to the top of the cardboard and pass it through the next slit, again in line with the bottom slit. Working to the right, continue feeding the yarn to the next slit on the reverse of the cardboard and feed from top to bottom and return from the bottom- to the top-aligned slits so that the warp yarns are straight. When you reach the last slit, holding the yarn in tension, tie the yarn in an overhand knot and secure through the last slit so that the knot sits on the reverse side of the loom.

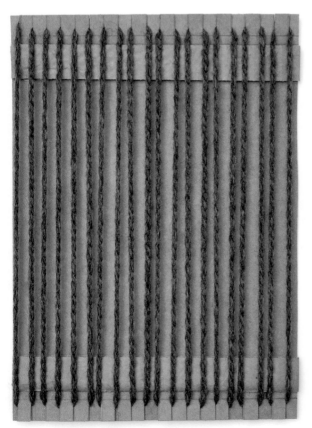

<u>7</u>

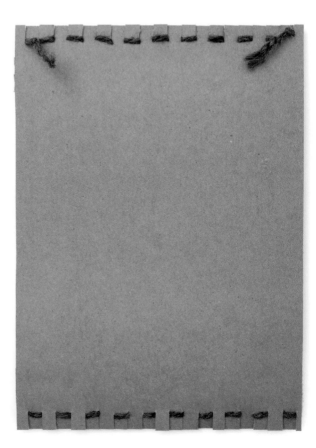

TOOLS OF THE TRADE

In this section, with its helpful visual guide, you'll learn about the tools that will prove most useful when you start frame-loom weaving.

---

1 & 2. STICK SHUTTLE

A stick shuttle is flat, rectangular, and notched at either end. The shuttle is used to hold a length of weft yarn as you pass it through the warp threads. It works best if it is longer than the width of the warp. Many varieties are available.

3. SHED STICK

A shed stick is used to select and lift particular warp threads and, when turned on its edge, provides a shed when weaving.

4. SWORD STICK

Used for the same purpose as a shed stick, the sword stick has a carved blunt blade and handle for ease of passing through warp threads. It can also be used as a beater or pick-up stick.

5. WEAVING COMB

Weaving combs are used to beat down the weft after each row of weaving. They are available in a range of different styles and sizes. Rather than buying a comb for this task, you can also use a kitchen fork.

6. FORK BEATER

Rather than purchasing a special weaving comb, you can use a kitchen fork instead, to beat down the weft threads while weaving.

7. TAPESTRY BOBBINS

Tapestry bobbins are small spools that are wound with weft yarn and used like a shuttle. They are useful for small areas of weaving, especially if combining sections of different wefts. The pointed end of a bobbin can be used to pick up warp threads and to beat the weft down tightly.

8. ROD

A rod is a very useful weaving tool. It is used for Looping (see *Rug-making Techniques*, pages 70–71), to make a leash rod (when weaving a large area of plain weave, using a rod and string is a more efficient way of picking up the alternate shed), and as a hanging device. A rod can easily be made from a piece of dowel.

9. DARNING NEEDLE

This is a long, blunt needle with a large eye, making it easier to thread with yarn. Darning needles and bodkins are used for finishing a piece of weaving with edging techniques such as hemstitching, fringing, and knot-and-darn edging.

10. NAALBINDING NEEDLE

A long flat, wooden needle with a large eye. It is used as the darning needle and is very suitable for frame loom weaving, especially when working with chunky yarns. It can also be used to weave across the warp. The name comes from a traditional Scandinavian technique.

11. TAPE MEASURE

12. RULER

13. SCISSORS

14. MASKING TAPE

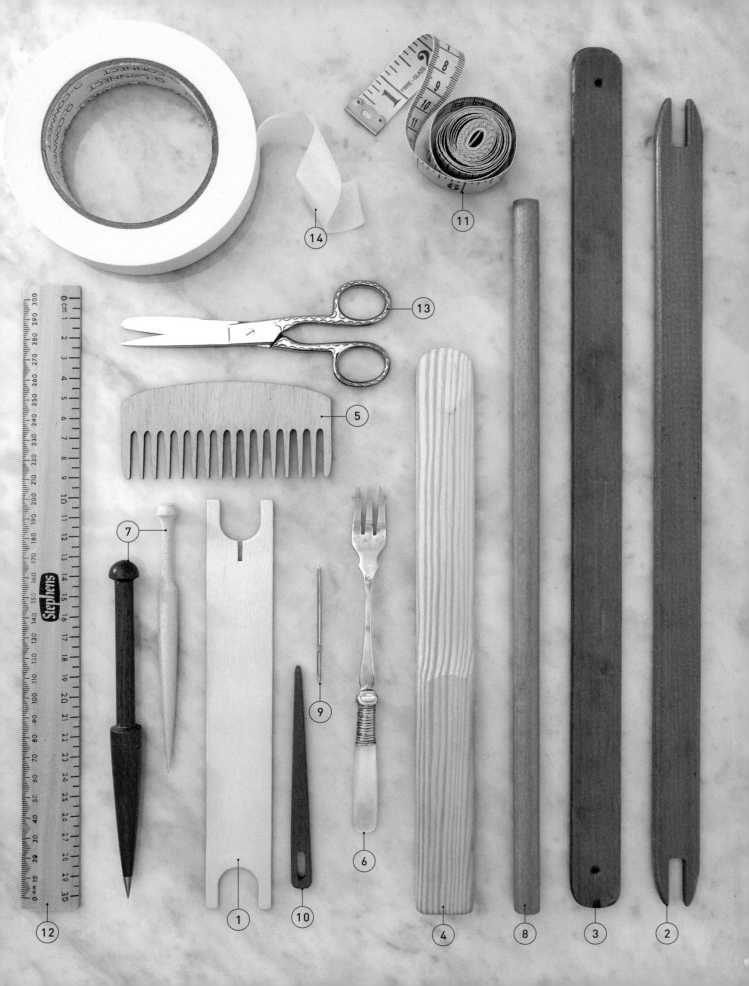

MEET THE MATERIALS

———

As Deb Chandler, weaver, weaving instructor, and author of Learning to Weave *puts it so simply, "Yarn is the raw material of fabric and fiber is the raw material of yarn."*

———

Your choice of yarn is so important to the overall finish of your woven project. This can be daunting for the beginner weaver, but a basic understanding and appreciation of different materials and fibers can help inform your yarn choice, with its suitability for a particular project in mind. Today, with such a wide variety of yarns available, learning a bit about the fibers from which they are made will help you to make your choice. Different fibers act in different ways, and experience will guide you in knowing how to handle each—for example, how the elasticity of wool would make a much more comfortable scarf than a stiff linen piece, which would be more suitable for a table runner.

FIBERS

The fiber that a yarn is made from will give it certain characteristics, as will the way it has been processed from fiber to yarn. Fibers can be categorized into five different groups: animal, plant, mineral, synthetic, and manmade. This book focuses on natural fibers, which are used in the project section. Natural fibers can be broken into two main categories: animal fibers and plant fibers.

Animal fibers are probably the ones that people are most familiar with, if only in name. These are the external growth on the animal and include wool, hair, down, fur, and fleece. They can all be shorn, without harming the living animal, and will regrow. They are therefore a renewable resource. Plant fibers are extracted from many parts of the plant, generally the stalk or leaves. For thousands of years, the fibers of animals and plants have been used to make cloth. It is only in the last century that synthetics and manmade fibers have developed. Our choice of fiber, however small, can have an impact on our natural environment and contribute toward a more sustainable industry.

This section looks at the most common natural fibers, and also some obscure ones, detailing each fiber's source, how it is grown, and its properties and uses. Included here is information on all the fibers used in the projects in the book, plus a few extra ones, including wool, angora, cotton, linen, bamboo, and nettle.

WOOL

Wool is the fiber that was originally used to make cloth. It is a broad term for describing the fiber that comes from the fleece of many different animals, such as goats, llamas, alpacas, camels, and, most commonly, sheep. While all are similar, I will focus on sheep's wool here. Thousands of breeds of sheep exist in the world, each with a wool that has many wonderful and varying characteristics. The fleece is shorn from the sheep annually, making it a sustainable, renewable fiber.

The fiber itself is hollow and cylindrical, with scales. It is these scales that give wool its unique insulating properties. Wool is extremely versatile and used for many applications, from fashion to floors to house insulation. There is so much I could say about the amazing properties of wool! It is a firm favorite with me and truly is "wonderwool"!

PROPERTIES:

- Warm—wool is the original fiber for warmth.
- Durable—extremely hardwearing, wool can withstand wear and tear over a long period.
- Stretch—wool has great elasticity.
- Naturally flame-retardant—wool is self-extinguishing. Untreated wool can withstand temperatures up to 1,058°F (570°C).
- Water-absorbent—wool can absorb 33 percent of its own weight in water, making it very suitable for Northern climates.
- Temperature regulator—wool will react to its environment or wearer.
- Insulating
- Hypoallergenic
- Static-resistant—unlike synthetics, wool is static-resistant, making it much more suitable for high-safety environments such as cars, airplanes, and trains.
- Bio-degradable

COTTON

Historically, cotton is regarded as "white gold" because it is the fiber that has created the most wealth and has been traded for centuries. Yet cotton is a relatively cheap crop and therefore a cheap fabric to produce. It is also extremely versatile, and is used in clothing, bedding, medical supplies, and even food!

The cotton plant is native to tropical and subtropical regions, such as the Americas, Africa, and India. Cotton fibers grow in little bolls on the stems of the bushy cotton plant, much like the fruit of the plant. A "boll" is a protective capsule around the seeds and is used for seed disperal. Each cotton boll only produces about ½ oz (14 g) of cotton. The fiber is soft and fluffy; it is also hollow and wilts when picked. The cotton fiber then collapses, curls, and shrivels, creating air pockets. These pockets are responsible for the fiber's warmth and softness. "Mercerized cotton" is cotton that has been processed to restore the fiber to its natural state—straightening the fiber and restoring its hollowness. This also makes the cotton shiny and reduces shrinkage in the finishing processes.

PROPERTIES:

- Non-allergenic
- Breathable
- Extremely soft
- Warm
- A heat conductor—cotton takes heat away from the body and therefore keeps the wearer cool. This is why it is so useful for summer fashion fabrics.
- Very strong

L I N E N

Linen is another historic textile, with its earliest written mention on tablets from Ancient Greece dating from 4,000 years ago. Linen comes from the flax plant. Flax is a tall plant that grows in a 100-day cycle and is planted annually. It has fine, spear-shaped leaves. The system of extracting the fibers from the stalk begins with retting, a process that involves soaking the flax stalks to stimulate bacterial growth. After this, the stalks are crushed with wooden blades to release the fibers within for spinning into yarn. Linen has no elasticity and so is not suitable for mixing with most other fibers, because of this lack of shrinkage. Cotton is the best blending partner for linen. In fact, yarns that are a blend of linen and cotton are quite common and excellent to work with.

PROPERTIES:

- Stiff—linen fiber has a "memory" and retains a shape.
- Cooling—linen is very suitable for summer wear.
- Breathable
- Light
- Very strong fiber—like all cellulose fibers, linen is even stronger when wet and so is particularly suitable for end purposes such as dish cloths, shower scrubbers, or muslins for straining food that will be constantly wet.

BAMBOO

Bamboo is a relatively new fiber in yarn production. There is much debate over the eco-friendliness of bamboo-yarn production. However, it is possible for bamboo to be processed naturally. The processing is similar to that of flax. Sadly, at present, most bamboo production is carried out chemically. This means that bamboo cannot strictly be categorized as a natural fiber, despite coming from a natural plant. As a result, it sits in the "manmade" category of fibers. The bamboo stalks are harvested, crushed, and chemically dissolved to form bamboo cellulose. These fibers are then spun into yarn. Bamboo fiber has a very long staple (see *Glossary*, pages 140–141, for explanation of staple.) It is hollow, allowing it to hold dyes more permanently, and is colorfast. Regardless of the bamboo-fiber production process, it is a fascinating fiber with many benefits.

PROPERTIES:

- Natural sterilization—used for medical purposes.
- Antibacterial and good moisture absorption—this makes bamboo fiber great for bathroom textiles and undergarments.
- Antidamp
- Very silky handle, lustrous
- Excellent drape—bamboo retains its shape, due to little shrinkage, making it suitable for clothing.
- Extremely strong
- Excellent durability—not likely to wear or fray

ANGORA

Angora is another type of animal fiber and is similar to wool. It comes from the fur of the angora rabbit. There are two types of angora hair: the coarse outer layer and the soft down inner coat. In angora yarn production, these two types of hair are combined. This creates a yarn with a characteristic of long, coarse, stiff hairs that occasionally protrude. Angora yarn is rare and more expensive than sheep's wool, yet it has many unique properties and advantages. It is eight times warmer than wool and can be used for lightweight warm garments. As angora has similar properties to wool, it is also often blended with wool.

NETTLE

The common European stinging nettle produces fibers that are suitable for yarn production. The fibers are white and silky, and can be up to 2 in. (5 cm) in length. During the two World Wars, nettle fiber was used as a replacement for cotton for clothing and army uniforms, due to shortages. Nettle fiber is finer than linen and can be as fine as cotton. A large advantage of nettle-fiber production, and also an area of continued research, is that nettle production requires less water than cotton. It could become a great substitute for cotton, as a sustainable crop in the future. And no, the yarn does not sting!

PROPERTIES:

- Eight times warmer than wool
- Absorbs less water than wool
- Felts easily
- Very soft, luxurious handle
- "Halo effect"—a characteristic of items made with angora yarn

PROPERTIES:

- Lightweight
- Quick-drying and resistant to mildew
- Lustrous
- Very little elasticity and therefore very strong
- Longevity—nettle has the longest lifespan of all the natural fibers.

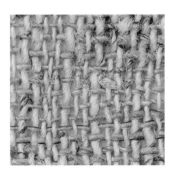

MORE ABOUT YARN

——

Yarn is a collection of fibers spun into a threadlike form. Two factors distinguish a yarn: its content (that is, which fiber or combination of fibers it is made of) and how the yarn has been constructed, which is what I look at in this section.

——

Yarn is constructed through a series of processes in which fibers are drawn out and twisted together to form a long, threadlike yarn. The first step in drawing out the fibers is called carding, after which the fibers can be combed to straighten them further. The process of twisting the drawn-out fibers together is called spinning. How a yarn is spun affects its characteristics. A yarn that is tightly spun, with a lot of twist, will be quite strong. A loosely spun yarn, with little twist, makes for a more fragile yarn.

PLYING AND THICKNESS

Once a single strand of yarn has been spun, it is often twisted around another strand. This is called plying. The plying of strands produces a much more stable and stronger yarn. The number of ply in a yarn is an indication of how many strands it is constructed with. For example, a 4-ply yarn is made up of four individual strands plied together. The thickness of the individual strands can also vary and this determines the overall thickness of the yarn.

All these processes can be done industrially in a textile mill or by hand using traditional techniques with hand carders and a spinning wheel.

YARN SIZE

There are so many different yarn count systems. I am often asked what is thicker than what and how to read certain systems. The truth is, there are so many systems out there that it is quite baffling! Different yarn count systems exist for different fibers and different industries, and even different manufacturers use different systems from country to country. As a hobbyist weaver, selecting yarn for your frame-loom projects, any yarn is suitable—just test it out! It is a myth that knitting yarn is not suitable for weaving. It is.

As you are more likely to be buying your yarn from a local yarn store than a large spinning mill, you'll probably be using knitting yarns sold in 2-oz (50-g) or 4-oz (100-g) balls. An important thing to note is that yarn is always measured and sold by weight. The length can vary and this may not even be included on the label. Knitters, and most yarn stores and suppliers, use a ply-weight system of yarn to describe its thickness. This can be misleading when you consider the process of plying—technically, a 4-ply yarn should be made of four strands of yarn and not determine the overall thickness of the yarn itself.

Don't worry if you feel overwhelmed by the various yarn count systems. A new universal system has been introduced as a solution. The NM (New Metric) System is an international yarn count system that aims to standardize yarn weights across the globe. It is based on scientific measurements. The chart below from www.yarnoncone.co.uk is a very useful guide to comparing both systems:

NM System	Ply Weight System
NM 1–1.3	Bulky weight
NM 1.3–1.8	Medium weight
NM 1.8–2.4	Worsted
NM 2.5–4.5	"4-ply"
NM 5–8	"3-ply"
NM 9–12	"2-ply"
NM 13–16	"1-ply"/laceweight
NM 16+	"Zero ply"/cobweb

Having said all that, the best way for a weaver to determine the thickness of a yarn for the purpose of weaving is to measure its e.p.i. (ends per inch), as explained in *A Project Plan* (see pages 32–35). Another solution is to wind off ¾ oz (20 g) of the yarn onto a finger skein (see page 45). Measure the length of this yarn. Then, by multiplying this length by five, you will know the length per 4 oz (100 g). This is useful for calculating the meterage of yarn in a 4-oz (100-g) ball.

HOW THE FRAME LOOM WORKS

———

The frame loom, as the name suggests, consists of a frame, usually rectangular, with two side bars, a base bar, and a top bar. Put simply, a loom is any device that can hold warp threads taut for weaving.

———

When warp threads are taut, they can be woven. The frame loom is held portrait, with the warp threads traveling from the top to the bottom. The frame loom I used in this book has a fixed warp. This means that the warp does not move once it is on the loom and the maximum length of the warp is determined by the size of the frame. This is usually three-quarters the height of the loom.

1. PEGS

The main purpose of the pegs across the top and base bars of the loom is to space the warp threads evenly across the width of the weaving. This helps to create a consistent cloth.

The pegs have a second purpose. The warp threads can be wound directly around each peg, instead of the frame itself—this is a simpler method to begin with.

2. DENT

The name given to the space between two pegs or nails on the frame loom.

3. WARP THREADS

The threads stretching vertically from the top bar to the base bar of the loom. These are wound around the frame loom under tension so that the weft can be woven through.

4. WEFT THREADS

The weft threads are woven under and over horizontally across the warp threads, creating patterns and structures in the weave.

5. SHED STICK

A shed stick is used to select and lift particular warp threads to make it easier to pass through a shuttle of weft yarn.

6. STICK SHUTTLE

A shuttle is flat, rectangular, and notched at either end. The shuttle is used to hold a length of weft yarn as you pass it through the warp threads. The shuttle works best if it is longer than the width of the warp.

7. HEADING CORDS

Heading cords are used to space the warp threads evenly and to provide a firm base upon which to begin weaving.

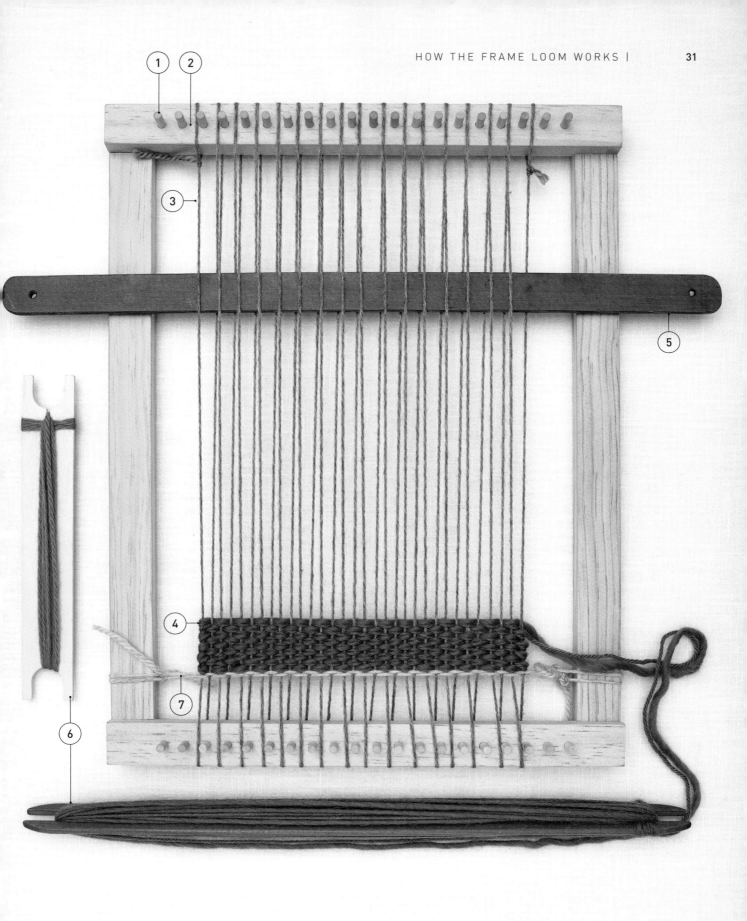

A PROJECT PLAN

———

In general, there is a known ratio among weavers that two-thirds of your time is spent preparing, while the remaining one-third is spent weaving. A project plan will help you to lay out all the information you need and consider how it is to be handled before you start weaving.

———

Although all the projects in this book have already been worked out in advance, this section is intended to equip you with the planning skills you will need to further explore the weaving techniques and structures showcased in *Chapter 2: Handweaving Techniques* (see pages 42–99). Hopefully, the guidelines given in this section will also encourage you to develop your own projects. A project plan consists of a design sketch and a spec sheet.

This is the Woven Wall Hanging (see *The Projects*, page 102), the design development for which is mapped out in the following pages.

THINGS TO CONSIDER BEFORE YOU START

Here are a few questions to get your creative mind working...

- What is the end piece to be?
- What is its function?
- What fiber is appropriate for this?
- What colors would suit?
- Which techniques will be used?
- What are the finished dimensions of the piece?

These inspirational images (left) were my starting point for this project. From these, I pulled colors that informed my yarn choices (below).

Below are some pages from my notebook, which develop ideas of form for both the Woven Wall Hanging and Foldover Purse (see *The Projects*, page 108).

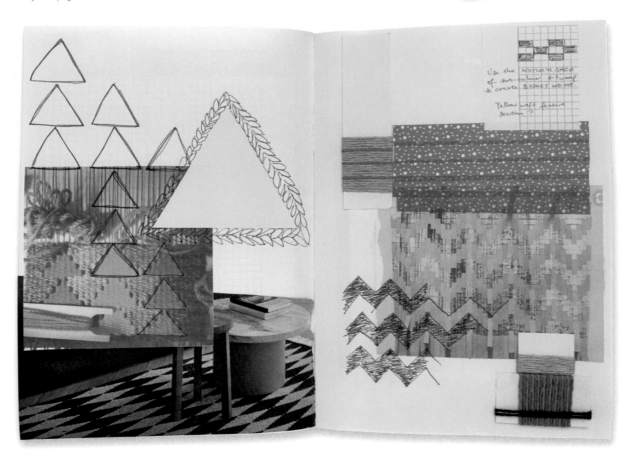

DESIGN SKETCH

The design sketch is an indication of how the piece will look. It helps you visualize the finished piece and how to go about making it.

In this design sketch, I have drawn out how I intend the finished woven piece to look. From this, I have an idea of how all the sections will look together and of the overall composition of the piece. This will help—in combination with the spec sheet (shown opposite)—when weaving my project.

YARN WRAPPINGS FOR WARP AND WEFT PLANNING

By wrapping yarns tightly around a piece of cardstock, you can get a feel for how different colors or yarns will interact with each other. Experiment with different color weighting and repetition. This can be done through color blending, or uniform or random stripes. This is useful when considering both warp and weft yarns.

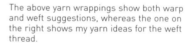

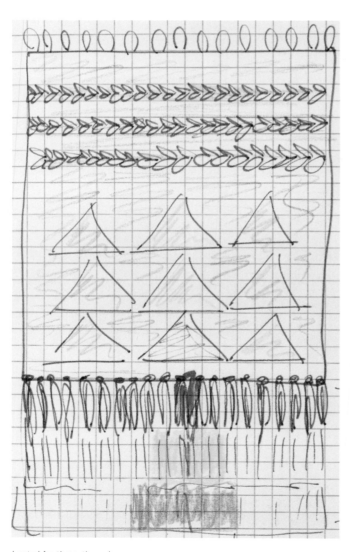

The above yarn wrappings show both warp and weft suggestions, whereas the one on the right shows my yarn ideas for the weft thread.

I opted for three-tier color fringing and incorporated a triangle into the design to reflect the shape used throughout.

RECORDING YOUR YARN

Yarn swatches are very important for recording which yarns you have used in a particular project. They are also helpful for keeping track of each yarn's color name, fiber, and brand, etc., as well as where you purchased it.

SPEC SHEET

A spec sheet is a useful part of the planning process because it consists of a record of all the technical details that are necessary for a particular project. This means that the project can then be repeated to the exact same specifications later on. The spec sheet includes information on woven measurements, yarns used, and calculations of warp and weft threads.

Warp Width: How wide will my project be?

Sett: How many "ends per inch" (known as e.p.i.) do I need?

The sett of a woven cloth refers to how many warp threads there are in every inch (2.5 cm). It indicates how tightly or loosely spaced the warp threads are, according to yarn thickness. This is worked out by calculating how many "ends per inch" there are (see below, right).

Total Warp Ends: (Warp Width X Sett)

Warp Length: (Height of Frame Loom + Depth of Frame)

Total Warp Yarn Needed: (Total Warp Ends X Warp Length)

Warp Yarns: Will the warp be in one yarn or a combination of yarns to add stripes to your design? If so, plan where the stripes will be and then calculate how wide and the number of warp ends accordingly.

Woven Length: Remember the maximum woven length of the piece will be three-quarters the height of the frame loom.

Total Weft Yarn Needed: (Warp Width X "Picks per inch" —p.p.i) X Length of Woven Piece. (p.p.i.—see below, left.)

PICKS PER INCH

A "pick" is a single weft row or shot of weaving. It can be useful to know the number of p.p.i. (picks per inch/2.5 cm), to ensure you have enough weft yarn. To calculate the p.p.i., count the number of weft shots in 1 in. (2.5 cm) in a sample. The sample must be woven in the same yarn, sett, and pattern.

ENDS PER INCH

Below are some examples of yarns in a variety of thicknesses, wrapped over 1 in. (2.5 cm) of cardstock. Note how the thicker yarn has fewer e.p.i. (ends per inch), and therefore a lower sett, than the finer yarn, which has more e.p.i. and thus a higher sett.

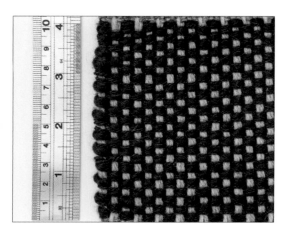

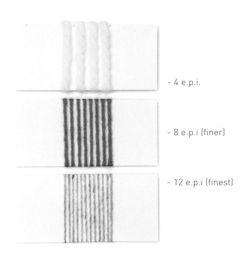

- 4 e.p.i.

- 8 e.p.i (finer)

- 12 e.p.i (finest)

SETTING UP THE FRAME LOOM

———

Having decided upon the sett, warp width, and choice of yarn for your project plan, you will begin setting up or "dressing the loom," as this stage is sometimes called. Essentially, to dress the loom, the warp is repeatedly wound around the frame in a figure eight until the desired number of warp threads is achieved.

———

1 Starting at the top of the loom, tie the warp yarn securely around the top bar in the first dent, using a Square Knot (see *Knots*, page 97). You will be working from left to right. Here, I started on the second dent in from the left and will finish on the second-last dent from the right. Tie the yarn so that the knot is placed close to the underside of the frame. The long tail attached to the ball of yarn should fall downward.

2 Bring the warp yarn down to the base of the frame, passing it over the front, as shown. Place the warp yarn in the dent that is parallel to the dent used directly above. Bring the warp yarn around the back of the frame and then pull it up into the internal space of the frame.

3 Pull the ball of yarn tightly up to the top bar of the frame. Pass the ball over the front of the top bar, placing one thread in the next dent immediately to the right of the first. Bring the ball to the back of the frame again. You have now wound two warp threads.

4 Working from left to right, continue winding the yarn from the top to the base bar, placing one thread in each dent (as it appears from the front) in a figure eight around the frame. Hold the warp yarn quite taut as you wind. You will begin to see the number of threads wound is doubled at the center of the internal space, where the threads have plateaued. This is the center of the figure eight where the warp threads have crossed over, and is called the cross (see below). If you need to count the warp threads, then count them at the cross.

5 Continue winding until you reach the last dent, which will be on the top bar. Holding the yarn in tension, cut it off with a 4-in. (10-cm) tail and tie it around the top bar, as you did at the beginning of the warp in Step 1. Tie the knot so that it sits quite close to the top bar. Secure with a double knot, maintaining the tension.

You have now finished warp winding! For a warp with a higher sett, the number of yarns per dent can be increased.

WARP WIDTH

Regardless of the warp width, the warp is always placed in the center of the frame. If the warp is narrower than the frame, then measure accordingly, to work out the first dent to be used.

4 THE CROSS

1

2

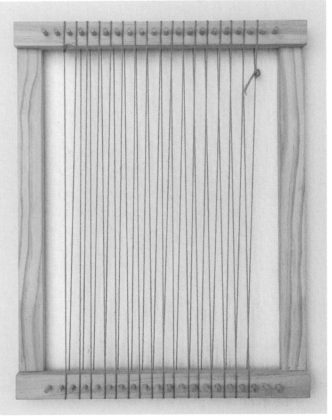

3

4–5

HEADING CORDS

For the heading cords, use either the same yarn that you used for the warp or a slightly thicker yarn. The yarn will be under a lot of tension, so it is advisable to choose a tightly spun yarn. Here are two different methods for setting up the heading cords. Woven heading cords are easier and quicker to set up, whereas clove hitch cords are a little more fiddly, but much more decorative!

WOVEN HEADING CORDS

1 Wind a finger skein (see page 45) of heading cord yarn to a length of two and a half times the width of the frame loom. Tie the yarn to the left-hand side bar of the frame, close to the base. Tie in a tight, secure Square Knot (see *Knots*, page 97).

2 Bring the finger skein above the cross of the warp threads and pass it through the natural shed (a). This is the triangular space that exists in the depth of the frame between the two sets of warp threads: those at the front of the frame and those at the back. A shed allows you to weave your shuttle through the warp threads. Then pass the finger skein from left to right, the whole way across to the right-hand side of the frame (b).

3 Pull the finger skein and heading cord down toward the base bar of the loom to wherever you want to begin weaving. You will notice that this brings the cross down with the heading cord and that the cord alternates under and over each warp thread.

4 Pull firmly on the heading cord, so that it is straight and sitting perpendicular to the warp. Use your fingers or a fork to help straighten it by beating downward. Tie the cord very tightly to the right-hand side bar. Again, tie in a secure Square Knot. The tighter the heading cord, the firmer the base you will have to weave on. Respace the warp threads evenly with your fingers, if necessary. Trim the tail from the heading cord to about ¾ in. (2 cm).

5 To weave the second heading cord, tie the finger skein to the frame once more, but this time to the right-hand side bar. Then pass the skein through the picked-up shed of the warp (using a shed stick). Beat the heading cord, as you did before, and then tie it securely to the left-hand side bar.

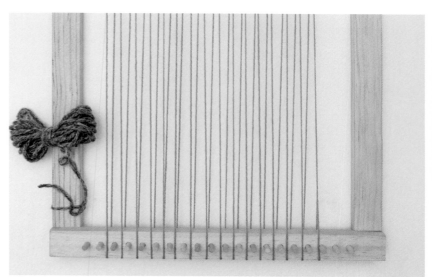

1

2a

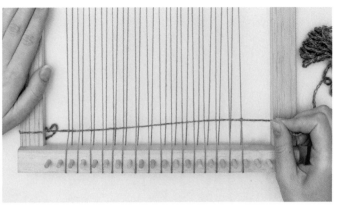

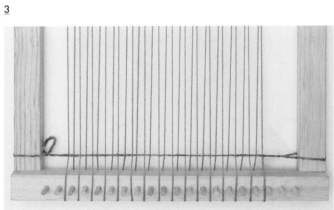

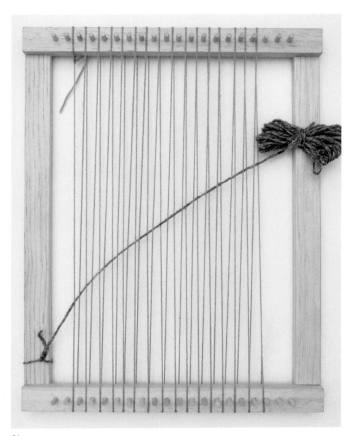

2b

3

4

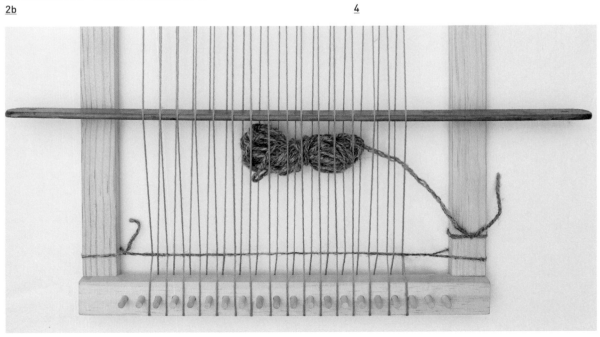

5

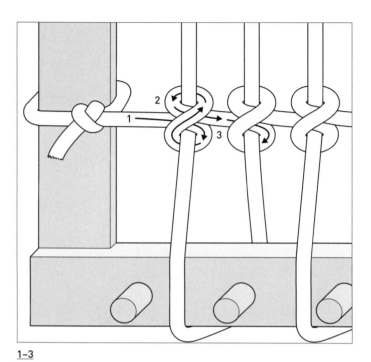

1-3

CLOVE HITCH CORDS

1 Wind a finger skein (see page 45) of heading cord yarn to a length of four times the width of the frame loom. Tie the yarn to the left-hand side bar, as you did for the *Woven Heading Cords*, page 38. Pass the yarn over the warp thread, from left to right.

2 Tuck the yarn under the warp thread, from right to left. Above this wrap, pass the yarn under the warp thread, again from right to left.

3 Before pulling tightly, pass the yarn under the long vertical loop that you just made in Step 2. Pull tightly into place.

4 Continue to tie a clove hitch knot around each individual warp thread, using the same continuous finger skein and moving from left to right. Make sure to maintain a consistent tension and equal distance between the warp threads. Tie off the yarn around the right-hand side bar, as before.

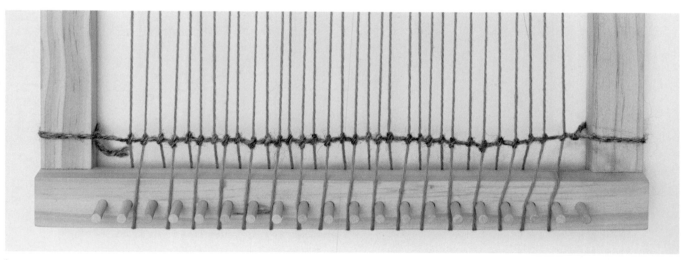

4

TENSIONING

While warp winding, a shed stick can be inserted or taped across the top rear of the frame loom to sit under the warp threads. When the warp threads become tight (i.e. toward the end of the weave), the stick can be removed and so ease the tension. This can also help to lengthen the warp. Similarly, a stick can also be added later to increase the tension, if the warp threads become too slack.

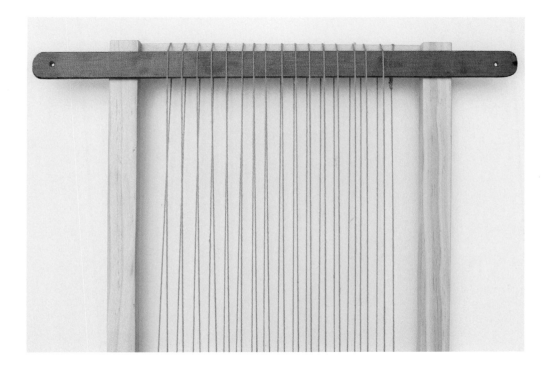

CHAPTER 2

HANDWEAVING
TECHNIQUES

CHOOSING THE RIGHT SHUTTLE

———

The frame loom is dressed; the warp is all set up. The next step is to prepare the weft before weaving with a shuttle. I use the term shuttle broadly to describe any device used to hold a length of weft yarn so that it can be woven. Here are three examples of different types of shuttle—each of which is useful in its own way—and instructions on how to wind them.

———

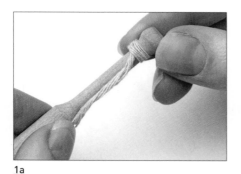

1a

1b

2a

2b

3

4

HOW TO WIND A TAPESTRY BOBBIN

A tapestry bobbin is useful for small areas of weaving, especially if you are combining sections of different wefts (see *Tapestry Techniques*, pages 50–63). It is also the ideal shuttle to use when weaving finer yarns. The pointed end of a bobbin can be used to pick up warp threads and for beating the weft down tightly.

1 Begin by holding the tail of yarn lengthwise along the shank of the bobbin, running upward from the handle to the head. Wrap the yarn tightly around the top of the shank (a) and then continue winding in a single layer until you reach the base of the shank (b).

2 Wind the yarn around the shank at an angle, this time moving upward from the handle to the head (a). Continue winding the yarn downward and then upward along the shank until it bulges just beyond the diameter of the handle and head (b).

3 Cut the yarn and tie off in a Half Hitch Knot (see *Knots*, page 97), as shown. This prevents the yarn tangling and unraveling.

4 Tying a Half Hitch Knot means that you should be able to hang the bobbin from a length of weft.

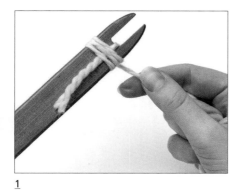

1

2

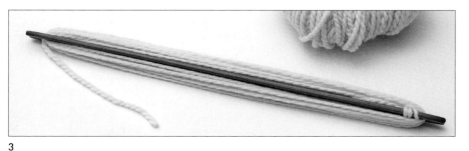

3

HOW TO WIND A STICK SHUTTLE

Used to hold a long length of weft, a stick shuttle is easy to pass through the warp.

1 Pointing the shuttle upward, place the tail end of the yarn through the indent. Wrap the yarn tightly around the shuttle a few times to hold the tail in place.

2 Bring the yarn through the indent once more, pull downward, and pass it through the indent at the other end of the shuttle. Bring the yarn back up and pass it through the first indent again. Wind the yarn from one indent to the other, wrapping it around the shuttle until it builds up on both sides.

3 Stop winding when you have enough yarn and cut the yarn from the ball. Don't overfill the shuttle, as it needs to be slender enough to fit through the shed.

1

2

3a

3b

4

HOW TO WIND A FINGER SKEIN

A finger skein is often called a butterfly. You don't need any special tools here—just your fingers and some yarn. A finger skein is very useful for shorter lengths of weft or for weaving multiple wefts. It is suitable for bulky wefts, as well as fine ones. You can easily change the size of a finger skein—just adjust your fingers.

1 Begin by passing the yarn between your thumb and index finger, leaving a tail to hang over the palm of your hand. Wrap the yarn around the outside of your thumb and pass it between your ring and baby fingers. Wind the yarn in a figure eight around your baby finger and thumb, as shown.

2 Fill up the skein by continuing to wind.

3 To tie off the yarn, bring the tail up over the top of the skein (a) and then pull it down on the inside to form a loop (b).

4 Bring the tail of the yarn over the skein and pass it through the loop. Pull tight. Cut the yarn from the ball, about a hand's span from the skein. To remove the skein from your hand, pull upward. When you start weaving, you will feed the yarn with the long tail.

HOW TO HAND WEAVE

—

After dressing the loom with warp threads, spacing with heading cords, and preparing a shuttle, you are ready to begin weaving. Here's how!

—

1 Pass the shuttle through the natural shed of the warp toward the top of the frame, where it is most open. Pass the shuttle from one selvage to the other, moving from right to left. On the first pick, hold on to the end of the weft yarn, keeping a tail of about 2.5 in. (6 cm) on the right-hand side. Tuck in the tail, as described in *Tucking Tails* (see page 49).

2 Pull the weft shot downward, to meet the previous pick or heading cords. With your finger, pull the weft up in the center to make an arc shape. This helps to stop the edges of your woven piece from pulling inward.

3 Using a beater or a kitchen fork, beat the weft shot into place so that it forms a straight line that is perpendicular to the warp and is sitting above the previous pick or heading cords. You've now completed one pick!

4 With the shed stick, pick up the next shed. In this example, we are weaving plain weave. The next shed will be the alternate shed. Insert the shed stick, so that the lower warp threads are raised over the stick and the higher warp threads are pushed below the stick. The stick will travel under one thread, over one thread, under the next thread, and over the following thread, alternating in this way across the whole warp to the left-hand selvage.

5 Once the shed stick has picked up the desired warp threads across the full width of the warp, push the stick downward to rest approximately 4 in. (10 cm) above the weaving (a). Now, twist the shed stick so that it is standing upright on its side (b). This further raises the warp threads and creates a decent shed space.

6 Pass the shuttle back through the shed, this time from left to right. The shuttle will always be passed back from the same selvage that you just finished on the previous pick. Make an arc shape, remove the shed stick, and beat, as before. Repeat Steps 1-6, to continue weaving.

1

2

<u>3</u>

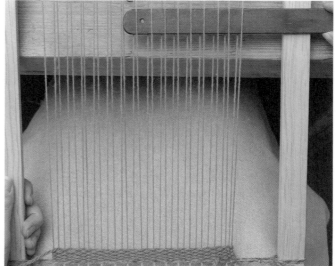

<u>4</u>

<u>5a</u>

<u>6</u>

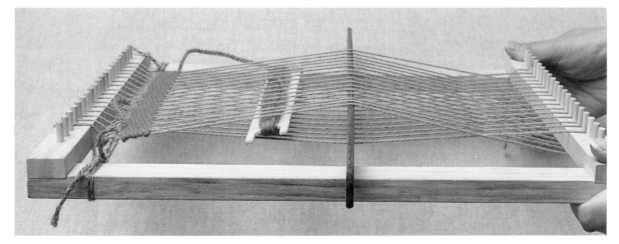

<u>5b</u> THE SHED

LEASH ROD

If you are weaving a large area of plain weave, using a leash rod and twine is a more efficient method of picking up the alternate shed.

YOU WILL NEED

Frame loom
Leash rod (longer than the width of the frame)
Finger skein of strong twine (at least four times the length of the warp width)
Stick shuttle of weft yarn

1 Place the rod on top of the warp threads, just below the upper bar of the frame. Tie the finger skein of twine to the left-hand end of the rod.

2 Thread the twine underneath the first warp thread (this will be in the lowered set) and back over the top of the rod, leaving about 1¼ in. (3 cm) between the warp thread and the rod. Continue threading under the lower warp threads and over the rod, skipping over the higher warp threads as you go. Continue across the entire width of the warp.

3 Carefully re-adjust the length of each leash, if necessary, so that they are all equal and the rod is straight. Tie the twine to the right-hand side of the rod.

4 To weave with the leash rod, pull the rod down to about 4 in. (10 cm) above the weaving. Pull the rod outward from the warp to raise the alternate shed and pass the shuttle through.

5 To weave the next pick, push the rod up to the top of the frame. The leashes should be long enough so that, when the rod is not lifted, the leashed warps are lowered. To weave, pass the shuttle through the natural shed of the warp.

Repeat Steps 4 and 5 to weave the desired number of picks in plain weave. See *Tucking Tails*, opposite, to finish your weft.

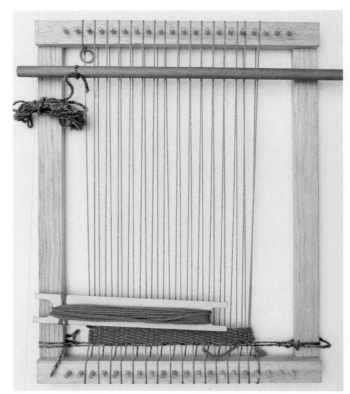

1

2

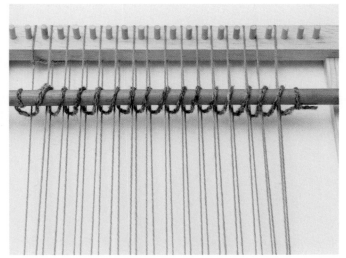

3

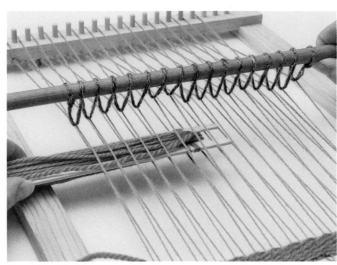

4

5

TUCKING TAILS

To start a weft, pass the shuttle through the shed, holding on to a 2½-in. (6-cm) tail of weft at the edge of the warp. Tuck the weft tail around the outermost warp thread (either under or over once, whichever is the opposite of the last shed you wove). Raise the same shed and bring the tail through the shed for a couple of inches, then pull it up to sit on top of the weaving. Beat as normal. Continue weaving.

To finish a weft yarn (i.e. when changing yarns or finishing a piece), cut the weft yarn about 2½ in. (6 cm) away from the selvage, after passing the shuttle through. Then tuck the tail, as described above.

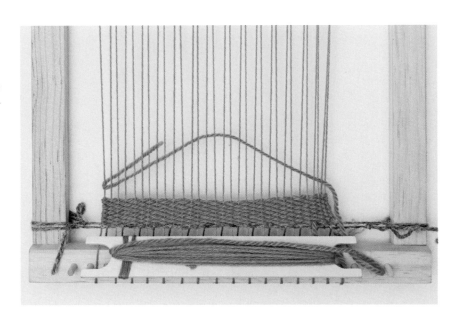

TAPESTRY TECHNIQUES

——

*The defining characteristic of a tapestry lies in its construction:
A tapestry is a weft-faced, plain-weave textile made up of small
patchwork-like areas of individual colored wefts to form a design or
image that is similar in appearance to a mosaic. In principle, unlike
other types of weaving, in a true tapestry a weft will never weave
entirely from one selvage to the other. Instead, multiple discontinuous
wefts collectively span the width of the warp. Typically, a tapestry is
most often used as a wall hanging or sometimes a soft furnishing. Purists
believe that a tapestry is only a true tapestry if it is a rectangular,
weft-faced, plain-weave piece of weaving with discontinuous wefts.*

——

Tapestries are typically woven on large high warp (vertical) or low warp
(horizontal) looms by teams of weavers working simultaneously. The process of
making a tapestry begins with a life-size drawing—known as a "cartoon"—of what
the tapestry will look like. The cartoon is placed behind the warp threads and
used as a guide for filling up the warp threads with specific colored wefts. Unlike
other forms of weaving, tapestry weavers work facing the reverse of the tapestry,
as it is easier to deal with weft tails from that position. This means that a tapestry
is woven as a mirror image of the finished piece. The final reveal of the tapestry
only occurs once it is finished and rolled off the loom.

This section is intended merely as an introduction to a handful of tapestry
techniques. I have chosen those that I think are essential for getting started and
to give you an appreciation of traditional tapestry weaving. *Joining Wefts: Vertical
Joins and Diagonals* (see pages 52–55) introduces methods to help you weave
successfully with multiple discontinuous wefts. *Making Curves, Angles, and Shapes*
(see pages 56–63) prepares you for creating your own designs in tapestry. The
shapes are accompanied by step-by-step instructions on how to weave a kilim-
style triangle and semicircle, with the aim of inspiring you to weave further
shapes in a tapestry style. As with all the techniques in this book, my advice for
the frame-loom weaver is to experiment and explore combining different
techniques—despite what the purists may say!

Tapestry weaving has its own terminology, so I have used those terms in this
section. As tapestry is always woven in plain weave and in a sequence of one pick
followed by a returning pick, two consecutive picks are called a "pass" and a
single pick is called a "half-pass."

JOINING WEFTS:
VERTICAL JOINS AND DIAGONALS

As tapestry designs are made up of different blocks of color and shapes, you need to learn how to weave with multiple wefts in order to create the desired effect. You will also have to know how to join these wefts, as they sit side by side in a tapestry. As the joining of wefts is so essential to tapestry weaving, many different techniques have developed. Each is useful for producing different outcomes. Choosing the most suitable technique to achieve the desired effect requires great skill and attention on the part of the tapestry weaver. A key thing to remember when joining wefts is to keep the passes on both wefts consistently in the same shed. This is so that, after weaving a block of joined wefts, it is still possible to weave one weft across the entire warp in the one shed. This section illustrates how to achieve a number of vertical joins and also a diagonal join.

NOTE: *Rugs can be made using tapestry techniques, primarily the kilim technique, from which the name for the kilim rug is derived. A kilim rug is, in fact, defined as a rug made using a tapestry technique! The term "kilim" refers to slit tapestry, which is woven with slit joins (see opposite).*

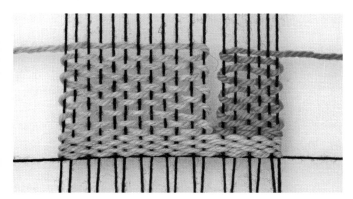

UNBEATEN

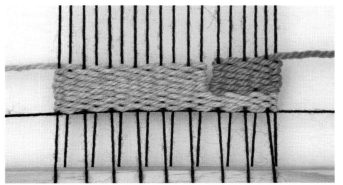

BEATEN

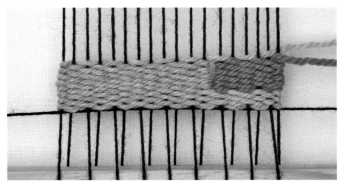

HALF-PASS RUNNING INWARD TO THE SLIT JOIN WITH ONE
CONTINUOUS WEFT SHOT AFTER SLIT JOIN

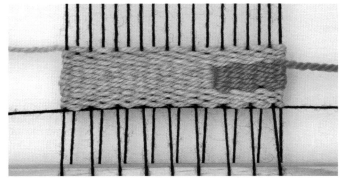

CONTINUOUS SEQUENCE OF PASSES

SLIT JOINS

A slit join involves weaving two wefts so that
they meet at adjacent warp threads before
being woven back in the opposite direction in
the next shed. The two wefts do not interlock.
After weaving in this way for several passes,
with the wefts repeatedly meeting at the same
warp threads, you will see a slit or gap appear
between the two blocks of weft.

This slit might be needed to create a subtle
outline on a shape or to add a different textured
line to the imagery in your tapestry. You could
even weave a bulky weft, a ribbon perhaps, in
and out of a series of slits. Generally, weaving
slit joins creates a very flat piece of weaving
with a sharp line. This style of weaving is called
"kilim" and results in flat, geometric designs.

Make sure to keep the tension slack on the
weft by making an arc (see Step 2, *How to Hand
Weave*, on page 46), especially on half-passes
outward from the slit. If the weft is pulled too
tight, the result will be a gaping hole, rather
than a subtle slit. Another option that is often
used for long slits is to stitch up the slits with
Soumak Stitch (see pages 68–69), thus outlining
the shape.

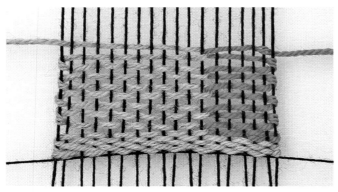

UNBEATEN

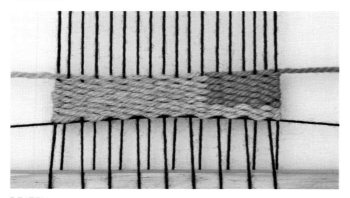

BEATEN

CLASPING

Like a slit join (see previous page), a clasped join involves weaving two wefts so that they meet at adjacent warp threads, only this time the two wefts are interlocked before you weave the next half-pass in the opposite direction.

To achieve this effect, weave both shuttles toward each other on the natural shed up to the warp threads where they are to meet. Pull both shuttles up to the surface of the weaving. Swap the shuttles over, clasping the wefts around each other. Insert the shed stick, picking up the opposite shed, and weave both shuttles back toward the selvages. Repeat this sequence for the required number of passes in order to make a block of the desired size. Then finish the weaving with an outward half-pass on both sides.

This technique creates a vertical join where all the wefts are fully interlocked. It is a very stable weave, with no risk of an open hole developing. However, it is more time-consuming than the slit-join method and creates a somewhat bulkier join. Use this method if you want a sturdy cloth with no holes.

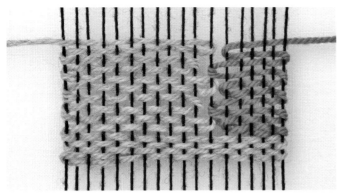

UNBEATEN

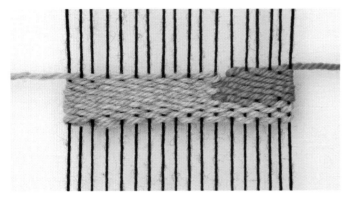

BEATEN

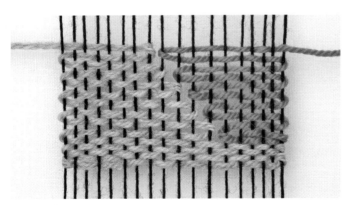

UNBEATEN

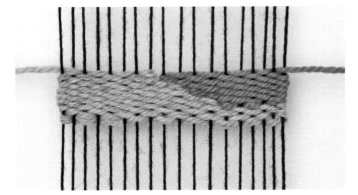

BEATEN

DOVETAILING

Dovetailing is similar to slit joins (see page 53) in that the wefts meet at adjacent warp threads and return outward on the next half-pass, without interlocking. The difference lies in the fact that the pair of warp threads where the wefts meet are staggered from pass to pass. A dovetail join is woven over three warp threads, A, B, and C. On the first row, the two wefts meet at the pair of warp threads, A and B. On the second row, the wefts meet at the second pair of warp threads, B and C. Note that warp thread B is always in a pair. This results in a staggered vertical join that is flush and has no slit. Bear in mind, however, that this technique is quite time-consuming. A tip to help you keep track of which pair of warp threads to stagger between is to mark the three warp threads with tape at the top of the frame and label them A, B, and C.

After testing out these different methods, you may begin to appreciate why most tapestries do not have many or large vertical joins, as most of them are very time-consuming or create a slit. For this reason, diagonals and curves are much more common in tapestry designs, and these are explained below and on the following pages.

DIAGONALS

Joining wefts on a diagonal is a good solution when you are dealing with multiple wefts and color variations, as it creates a clean, straight, neat, flat join. There are no slits or extra bulk, and it is easier to keep track of the warps than in dovetailing.

Weave two weft yarns toward each other to meet at two particular warp threads, A and B. Pull both shuttles to the surface of the weaving. Change the shed by picking up alternate warp threads with a shed stick. Weave the shuttles back in opposite directions to the selvages. When weaving a rightward diagonal join, shift the meeting point of the wefts by one warp thread to the right on each half pass. This will result in the left-hand weft gradually growing longer while the right-hand weft decreases on each row. For a leftward diagonal (as shown left), shift the meeting point one warp thread to the left on each row.

MAKING CURVES, ANGLES, AND SHAPES

Once you have mastered diagonal joins, a simple variation of this technique will introduce curves and angles to your weaving repertoire. Since all shapes are formed from curves and angles, it therefore follows that you will then have all the necessary skills to make lots of different shapes, too. This section takes a close look at how curves are constructed. It also includes an introduction to creating shapes, which draws on the knowledge you've gained from weaving joins, diagonals, and curves. Included in this section are step-by-step instructions for weaving a triangle and a semicircle. These are intended as a first step in weaving different shapes. After completing these successfully, my hope is that they will inspire you to weave other forms and shapes. From weaving the semicircle, you could progress to weaving a full circle or a group of semicircles, while from triangles you might move on to combining pointed triangles with semicircles to form scallops, to name but a few ideas! Let's have a look at curves first.

CURVES

A curve is a continuously bending line, which veers from being straight, whereas a diagonal is always a straight line. To make a line bend, the shift of the meeting point of the two wefts must be altered. Previously, when weaving diagonals (see page 55), the shift was always equal—one warp thread to the right or left, and so on. The difference here lies in altering the shift of the "meeting point" of the two wefts between successive passes. It can be explained as consisting of deep and shallow steps on passes of the weft. For example, on one pass, weft A might extend two or three warp threads beyond where it traveled to on the previous pass—this would be a "deep step." On the next pass, it may only extend one warp thread beyond, which is called a "shallow step." Deep and shallow steps combine to form the arc of the desired curve. The sweep of the curve can be varied through the sequence of deep and shallow steps.

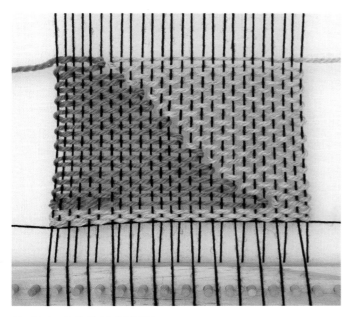

GRADUAL CURVE, UNBEATEN

A more gradual curve is created by weaving single passes of each step, alternating shallow and deep steps.

GRADUAL CURVE AFTER BEATING

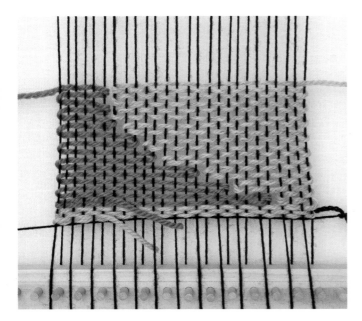

ROUNDED CURVE, UNBEATEN

For a more rounded curve, repeat some of the same "deep-step" passes, but punctuate them with a single "shallow-step" pass to smooth out the curve.

ROUNDED CURVE AFTER BEATING

TRIANGLES

Weaving a triangle involves weaving two diagonal joins at angles to each other, so that they meet at a point. Depending on the scale of the triangle, you may need to repeat passes to give the triangle height with distinct proportions. By repeating passes, slit joins (see page 53) are created with the next tier interlocked with the warp. This produces a kilim-style effect.

In this example, the triangle is worked over seven warp threads. The sett is 4 e.p.i. (ends per inch/2.5 cm). Each tier of the triangle is repeated over three passes, resulting in small slits. The triangle decreases by two warp threads on each tier, until the point of each triangle comes to a single warp thread.

With the repeated passes of each tier, the resulting triangle will hopefully be a handsome equilateral, depending on the neatness of the beating! This equilateral triangle is used in the *Woven Wall Hanging* (see pages 102–107), where it is woven in rows of three. To weave a larger triangle, the same principle applies, but you need to begin with a larger number of warp threads. Tip: Working with an uneven number of warp threads will ensure it can be decreased to a single thread for the point.

YOU WILL NEED

Frame loom

Shed stick

Beater/fork

Finger skein of weft yarn A, for the triangle weft

Finger skein of weft yarn B, for the left-hand background weft

Stick shuttle of weft yarn B, for the right-hand background weft

1 Select the seven warp threads for the base of the triangle, leaving space for four warp threads to the left to form the background and the desired number of warp threads to the right to form the right-hand background. Weave across these seven warp threads in weft A, using plain weave and tucking the weft tail to the back of the piece at the beginning. Repeat, weaving through seven warps for the next three passes in plain weave. Beat firmly after each half-pass, so that the warp thread is not visible.

2 Weave the background at the same time as the triangle to achieve a consistent weave. For the left-hand background, weave the finger skein with weft B through the four empty warp threads, continuing in the same shed you wove on the first half-pass in the triangle. Tuck the weft tail to the reverse of the piece at the beginning, as before. Weave in plain weave for three passes. Using the stick shuttle, weave the right-hand background with weft B in the same way. Weave for three passes, as you did for the other two sections.

3 To begin the next tier of the triangle, the number of warp threads woven will be decreased. Using weft A, weave across six warp threads on the first half-pass (a). Decrease to

weave across five warp threads on the returning half-pass. Repeat, weaving over these five warps for the next two passes (b). Beat firmly after each half-pass, as before.

4 Weave the left-hand background with the finger skein of weft B, increasing to weave over five warp threads, so that there is no empty warp between the triangle and the background. Weave for a total of three passes. Weave the right-hand background in the same way with the stick shuttle, increasing the weft to cover one extra warp thread and leaving no gap, as you did for the left-hand side. Again, weave for a total of three passes. The first two tiers of the triangle and both backgrounds are now complete.

5 For the next tier of the triangle, decrease weft A to weave over four warps on the first half-pass. Further decrease to weave across three warp threads on the returning half-pass. Repeat, weaving over these three warps for the next two passes. Beat firmly after each half-pass, as before. Similarly, with both background sections, weave weft B to increase by one warp on the first half-pass. Repeat, weaving across this number of warp threads for a total of three passes. Beat firmly.

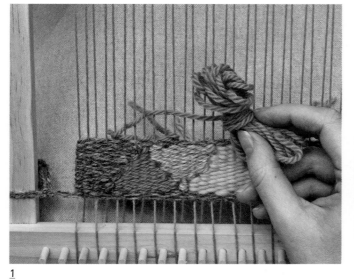

1

2

3a

3b

4

5

Continued overleaf

6

7

8

6 The last tier of the triangle forms the point. At the point of the triangle, wrap weft A around the single remaining warp thread three times and secure with a Half Hitch Knot (see *Knots*, page 97), as shown.

7 Draw the yarn down tightly to form the last tier of the triangle. Pull the weft tail to the reverse of the piece.

8 To complete both background sections, weave weft B to increase by one warp thread on both sides. Weave both left- and right-hand sides for three passes. After completing all three sections (i.e. the left-hand background, the triangle, and the right-hand background), it should be possible to weave across the entire warp in the same shed in weft B, as illustrated in the photograph.

Tapestry bobbins are fantastic for this system of weaving because you can use them both for picking up the warp threads and for beating. Finger skeins also work well. If you are weaving with multiple wefts, it is better practice to weave each tier of each shape simultaneously to build up the shapes and backgrounds across the warp. This will help you to keep the tension consistent across the piece, but also to keep track of the sheds across the warp. Remember that at any one point, it should be possible to weave one weft across the warp in the same shed. If not, there is a mistake and it is not a true tapestry!

SEMICIRCLES

A semicircle is essentially a large, 180-degree curve with a flat base. A curve-joining technique is used in the construction of this shape, using deep and shallow steps. The semicircle in this sample is worked over 26 warp threads set at 4 e.p.i. (ends per inch/2.5 cm). The more warp threads in the semicircle, the smoother the shape will be. The fewer warp threads, the more kilim-esque the shape will be.

This sample uses repeated passes and slit joins, in a similar way to the triangles opposite. The best method to achieve curved shapes, such as semicircles, in tapestry weaving is to use a "cartoon." The cartoon assists in "inking on," a technique that is described below. The same method can also be used for other shapes and more elaborate designs.

1 To make the cartoon, draw your semicircle to scale on a sheet of paper. You can use a circular object, such as a cup or side plate, as a template. Draw a horizontal line through the center. Center the cartoon underneath the dressed loom, flat on a table. (Prop up the cartoon with a book if necessary—the cartoon should sit almost flush with the warp threads, so that the warp and paper are touching.)

2 Using the felt-tip pen or marker, dot the warp threads following the shape of the cartoon. Roll the warp threads as you do so, to ensure you ink the entire circumference of each thread. The dots will be your guide for weaving. Essentially, you will fill in this shape in weft A and fill up the outside with weft B. Your inking on is complete.

YOU WILL NEED

Frame loom

Sheet of paper

Cup or side plate, for drawing the shape

Book, for propping up the cartoon (optional)

Felt-tip pen or marker

Shed stick

Beater/fork

Stick shuttle of weft yarn A, for the semicircle weft

Two finger skeins or stick shuttles of weft yarn B, for the left-hand and right-hand background wefts

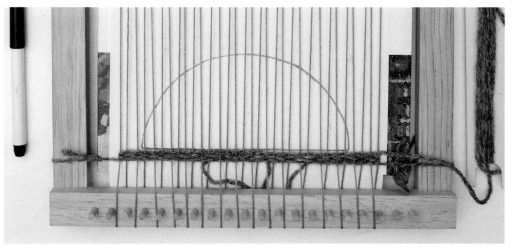

1

2

Continued overleaf

3

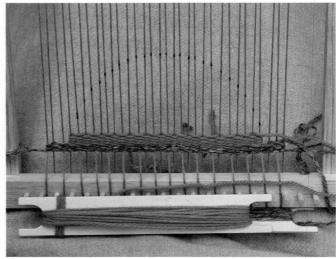

4

5

3 After weaving a few passes in weft B, across the entire warp, begin weaving the semicircle in weft A. Weave in plain weave across the center-most 26 warp threads, as indicated by the first pair of inked dots. (On this sample, there are 32 warp ends, to leave three empty warp ends on each side of the semicircle.)

4 Continue weaving back and forth across the full 26 warp ends in weft A, until you reach the next pair of dots on the warp ends. Decrease the number of warp threads woven accordingly. The dotted marks should be covered with weft A, so make sure to weave around these warp threads to include them in the semicircle shape.

5 For a more consistent weave, weave the shape and the background simultaneously. After weaving about a third of the semicircle in weft A, begin weaving the background sections on either side in weft B, using two separate finger skeins or shuttles. Begin weaving the background in the same shed as the first half-pass of the semicircle on the three remaining empty warp threads on each side. Weave for several passes, increasing the number of warp threads woven in weft B to correlate with the number decreased from the semicircle. Ensure that no warp threads lie empty between the semicircle and the background. Weave the background up to the same height as weft A in the semicircle. Make sure to finish on the same shed as the last half-pass of weft A.

6

7

8

6 Return to weaving the next third of the semicircle in weft A. As before, use the dots as a guide to decreasing the warp threads included in the shape. Note that this section will have fewer repeated passes and more frequent decreases, as the curve grows with shallower steps as you near the cusp. Weave up the background sections in weft B to match weft A, the semicircle, as you did in Step 5.

7 For the final section of the semicircle, weave weft A following the guideline provided by the dots. To form the cusp of the semicircle, weave single passes with deep steps, decreasing by two threads at a time. Keep track of the decreases to ensure that the curve is centered on the warp threads to produce a symmetrical shape. Check this by counting the empty warp threads on each side of the semicircle. The final half-pass of the semicircle is woven across six warp threads. This straight line magically creates the illusion of a curve once the background is woven around it. Do not be tempted to decrease the semicircle any further, as this will create a point, not a curve!

8 Weave up the final sections of the background in weft B. As before, increase weft B to correlate with the decrease of weft A. Make sure to keep consistently within the same shed as the semicircle. The final half-pass of the background should be worked over 13 warp ends on either side. Tuck one weft B tail to the reverse. With the other weft B, weave across the entire warp. It should be possible to weave from selvage to selvage in the one shed.

RUG-MAKING TECHNIQUES

———

A rug is defined as a piece of textile that lies flat on the ground or floor. It is a functional piece that must cover the floor and be protective, highly durable, and hardwearing enough to go underfoot. A rug is also insulating, adding warmth and softness to a room, and often decorative.

———

History shows that mankind has felt the need to cover the floors of dwelling places with a durable, patterned textile for at least 2,500 years! The word "rug" dates from the mid-16th century and probably originates from Scandinavia, being derived either from the Norwegian *rugga*, which means "coverlet," or the Swedish *rugg*, meaning "ruffled hair."

As rugs have been in existence for millennia, rug-making techniques have been honed and developed with some skill. However, these techniques are not limited to rug making, but can also be used in other types of weaving. They are perfect for using on a frame loom with brilliant results. The techniques described in this section are rya knots, soumak stitch, and looping. All these techniques create raised surface decoration, which is textured and also fun to do. Rya knots have a Northern influence with a dense, multistranded, high pile. Soumak stitch, as the name suggests, involves stitching the weft yarn around the warp. Looping involves making loops with a supplementary weft. Each technique can be easily varied by changing the yarn thickness or color and by varying the scale of each knot, stitch, or loop. These techniques can also all be combined with each other, as well as with areas of patterned weaving. They are beautifully showcased in some of the projects that feature later in the book.

RYA KNOTS

The rya knot originates in Scandinavia and is traditionally used to make heavily piled rugs, usually of thick, coarse wool to mimic the heavy furs needed for warmth in the region. The word *rya* means "rug" in Scandinavia and refers specifically to this type of rug. It is possibly derived from Ryafår, a breed of Swedish sheep whose long wool is thought to have been traditionally used to make this rug.

The rya-knot technique is extremely versatile. It can be used to make a single knot or row of knots to add raised surface decoration to weaving or as an edging technique to create decorative fringing. It can also be used for an entire piece, to create a densely textured rug effect. You can experiment with varying yarn thicknesses and pile lengths to create different effects. In between each row of rya knots, you will have to weave one or two rows of plain weave (see *How To Hand Weave*, pages 46–47) to keep your piece stable. I really love using the rya-knot technique, as it is a simple way of adding texture to a piece, easy to accomplish, and excellent for showing off beautiful yarns, especially homespun!

YOU WILL NEED

Frame loom
Scissors
Stick shuttle
Yarn for ground weft (plain weave)
Any type of yarn, for the rya knots

RYA KNOTS

In this sample, I wove two lines of plain weave at the beginning to provide a firm base for the rya knots to sit on.

1 After cutting some strands of yarn to the desired length, pick up four warp threads with your left hand. Place the yarn on top of the four warp threads so that the mid-point of the yarn is in the center of the raised threads.

2 With your right hand, tuck the right-hand ends of yarn under the two warp threads on the right. Pull the yarn up to the surface of the warp and leave to rest on the right-hand side.

3 Repeat this process, but this time tucking with the left-hand ends of yarn. Tuck the yarn under the two warp threads on the left-hand side, then pull the strands to the top in the center. This creates a horizontal float across the four warp threads, with the tails below creating the pile.

4 Pull both ends of yarn tight so that the rya knot is sitting on the warp threads. Then draw the ends down toward you to place the knot on top of the plain weave. Repeat to create a row of rya knots. Trim the piles to the desired length.

1

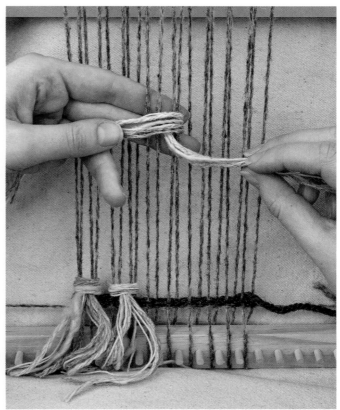

2

3

4

SOUMAK STITCH

The origin of soumak weaving is not certain, but it is thought to be from the Caucasus region—rugs and bags woven entirely of soumak stitch and dating from the pre-19th century have been found in this area. Some sources suggest that the name is derived from the Arabic word for a red dyestuff called "dyer's sumach." Regardless of the uncertainty surrounding its origins, soumak stitch is another traditional rug-making technique that's adopted all over the world and much used today.

Soumak stitch uses a continuous weft thread that loops around a group of warp threads, traveling from one stitch to the next, to create a raised texture or ridge. It reminds me of hand embroidery. A single row of soumak weaving creates raised slanted stitches. However, when you weave two lines together, slanting them in opposite directions, then something exciting happens—it creates a braided effect.

Remember, soumak stitch does not always have to be linear; it can also be used in a curve to outline a shape (see *Making Curves, Angles, and Shapes,* pages 56–57) or to create organic, wavy shapes across a piece of weaving.

YOU WILL NEED

Frame loom
Beater/fork
Finger skein of weft yarn (at least four times the length of the warp width)
Stick shuttle
Yarn for ground weft (plain weave)

1 Fold over the end of the weft yarn by 2 in. (5 cm). Tie this loop to the first warp thread on the right-hand side using a Lark's Head Knot (see *Knots,* page 97). Begin working in the direction of the tails (moving from right to left). Tuck the short tail to the reverse side of the weaving.

2 With your fingers, lift up the next two warp threads to the left. Pass the finger skein underneath these two warp threads and then pull up to the right side of the weaving once more.

3 Draw the stitch down toward the completed weaving.

4 Lift up the next two warp threads to the left and tuck the finger skein under again. Tuck so that the weft travels over four warp threads and back under two.

5 Continue in this way until you reach the last warp thread. Adjust the size of the stitches as you go, if necessary. You will see that this creates a stitch that slants upward to the right. (Soumak stitch always slants in the opposite direction to the one in which you are working.)

6 When you reach the end of the row, wrap the weft once around the last warp thread.

7 To complete the braid with the slant going in the opposite direction, you will need to weave another row of soumak stitch. Lift up the next two warp threads to the right. Pass the weft over these two threads, then tuck the weft back under the raised warp threads toward the left again.

8 Continue across the row, as you did before, so that the weft travels over four warp threads and back under two. The new direction you are working in changes the direction of the slant. To finish, wrap the weft once around the last warp thread on the right and tuck it to the back.

It is a good idea to weave one pick of plain weave between each soumak braid as a structural weft—in this example, I used a gray yarn to do this.

1

2

3

4

5

6

8

LOOPING

As the name suggests, looping is a technique that's used to make a series of loops across the weft by raising and extending the weft yarn into loops. It forms another type of pile and, unlike rya knots, the ends are looped together instead of being open ended. It can be used to create a dense rug effect, with rows of plain weave alternating throughout the piece to strengthen the cloth.

The challenge with looping lies in the consistency of the loops and their composition. Points to consider would be: Do you want the loops to form ordered vertical lines? If so, you must always repeat the loops over the same warp threads on each row. Do you want the loops to have a messy pile effect? If this is the case, stagger the loops. Do you want the loops to be uniform in size? If so, always loop around the same tool as your guide.

Why not use the looping technique to create a raised surface shape in a wall hanging? Combine it with soumak stitch or rya knots to outline the shape!

YOU WILL NEED

Frame loom
Pair of rods of the same size
Stick shuttle
Shed stick
Beater/fork
Yarn for ground weft (plain weave)
Finger skein of yarn, for looping

In this sequence, rod A is already in place as the looping is already in progress. For the purpose of this tutorial, we will begin using rod B. Once you have completed the sequence, you will understand how rod A and rod B alternate to make each looped row.

1 Pass the finger skein of yarn through the alternate shed of plain weave, using the shed stick to pick up the warp threads.

2 Working in the direction of the weft, pull up and loop each weft float around rod B. Loop around rod B in such a way that the weft spirals around rod B across the width of the warp threads.

3 Continue looping across to the end of the row. Push rod B so that it is sitting centrally on the warp. Leave rod B in place.

4 Weave the next row of plain weave using the ground weft yarn on the stick shuttle. This will be the natural shed, as it is the opposite shed to the one you just wove on the looped row. Beat.

5 Leaving rod B in place, remove rod A.

6 Beat the loops and plain-weave picks once rod A has been removed. Beat according to how dense you want the loops to be.

Repeat Steps 1–6, using rod A in the next sequence and rod B in the subsequent one. Repeat for the desired number of rows, alternating between using rod A and rod B. Finish with two rows of plain weave.

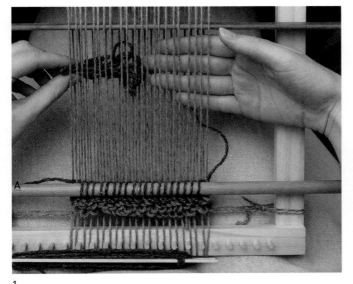

1

2

3

4

5

6

AN INTRODUCTION TO WEAVE STRUCTURES

Until this point, when weaving with a shed stick, I have only dealt with how to create plain weave, alternating two sheds. This section demonstrates how to introduce pattern into flat weaving.

Patterned weaving is achieved by picking up different combinations of adjacent warp threads in each shed. As I explained in the first chapter, the weaving process involves two sets of threads, vertical and horizontal, which interlace with each other. The sequence of these interlacements is what defines a weave structure. The weave structures in this book are based on traditional weaving using shaft looms, either table or floor, and are read from a weaving draft. In this section you will learn about plain weave, twill, herringbone weave, basket weave, rib, and traditional bird's eye.

A weaving draft is essentially a diagram of the woven pattern, showing the interlacements of warp and weft threads. It also indicates which threads need to lie on the surface to achieve this desired pattern. A full weaving draft includes a "threading sequence" for the warp threads, as these are individually connected to one particular shaft. It also includes a "lift plan" to show which warp threads to lift in combination across each shed. As there are no shafts in frame-loom weaving, the draft can be simplified and yet still achieve the desired woven pattern. The focus is on the remaining part of the draft, which is known as the "drawdown" (this is explained opposite).

This photograph shows how the shed stick is passed over two warps, under two warps, then over two warps, and so on in the first row of twill, ready for raising the shed.

WARP

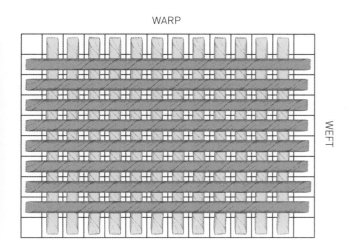

WEFT

WARP

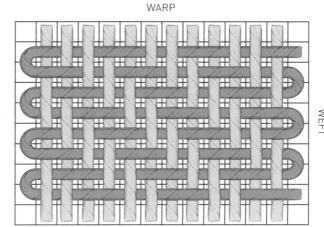

WEFT

Take a look at the grid, above left. The spaces between the lines represent the threads. All the columns are the warp threads and all the rows are the weft threads. In order for a weft thread to be visible, it must lie over a warp thread. Equally, when a warp thread is to be visible, it must lie over a weft thread. Therefore, the warp thread must lie on the surface, meaning that the weft thread must pass under it (see above right).

The diagram below is an example of a complete drawdown for Twill. The shaded boxes represent the weft and the blank boxes represent the warp, as indicated in the side and top bars. The shaded boxes show where the weft threads are visible on the surface. Across the same row, the blank boxes show where the warp thread is visible and the weft is not. This means that the weft thread travels under the warp threads in the blank boxes and resurfaces at the next shaded box. To put it simply, a shaded box indicates that you should pass the shuttle over a warp, while a blank box indicates that it should be passed under a warp. Inserting the shed stick in this manner will help to raise the correct warp threads in each shed, as shown in the photograph opposite.

DRAWDOWN

The numbers across the bottom of the drawdown refer to the warp threads and indicate the repeat of the sequence.

Always read the drawdown from the bottom row upward. This is so that the pattern builds in the same way moving upward, as you weave it on the loom. Read from right to left.

WARP

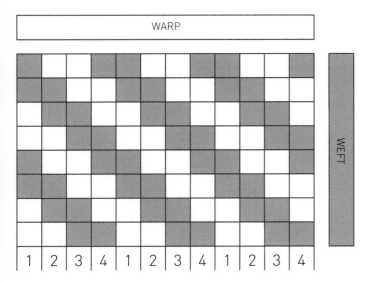

WEFT

| 1 | 2 | 3 | 4 | 1 | 2 | 3 | 4 | 1 | 2 | 3 | 4 |

This drawdown example for a twill weave could be read as follows: in the first shed, all #1 and #2 warps are to be lifted. In the second shed, all #1 and #4 warps are to be lifted. In the third shed, all #3 and #4 warps are to be lifted. In the fourth shed, all #2 and #3 warps are to be lifted. This sequence is then repeated over the desired number of picks. However, it is probably easier to think of it as follows: working from right to left in the first shed, the shed stick passes over two warp threads, under two warp threads, and then repeats in this way across the row. In the second shed, the shed stick passes under one warp, over two, and then under two, over two for the rest of the row. In the third shed, the shed stick passes under two warp threads, over two, and this is then repeated across the row. For the fourth shed, it passes over one warp, under two warps, and then repeatedly over two, under two until the end of the row.

PLAIN WEAVE

Plain weave is the simplest and most basic of weave structures. It produces the flattest and most even cloth. Also known as "tabby," plain weave is the most structurally sound weave because it has the highest interlacements of warp and weft threads. It involves alternating the warp and weft on every thread. The weft always travels under one warp thread, over the next warp thread, under the following warp, and over the next, and then continues to alternate in this way across the warp. On the next pick, for every warp thread that the weft went under on the previous pick, the weft now goes over that warp. Again, this sequence then alternates across the rest of the pick. All floats in plain weave are only ever one thread long. Despite being the simplest weave structure, plain weave can increase in complexity. For example, altering the balance of the cloth, perhaps by making it evenly balanced, weft-faced, or warp-faced, and using different colors can change the appearance of plain weave quite dramatically.

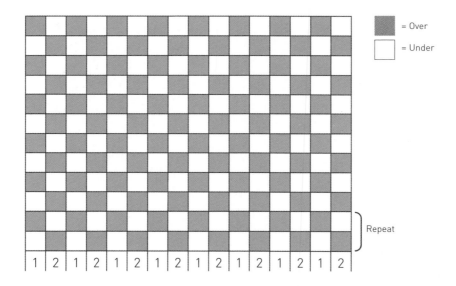

= Over

= Under

Repeat

| 1 | 2 | 1 | 2 | 1 | 2 | 1 | 2 | 1 | 2 | 1 | 2 | 1 | 2 | 1 | 2 | 1 | 2 |

WEAVE CHART

This should be read from bottom to top, right to left. After the second line, the pattern repeats.

A balanced weave is one in which the e.p.i. (ends per inch/2.5 cm) and p.p.i (picks per inch/2.5 cm) are equal in number. When the warp is set tighter than the p.p.i., the result is a warp-faced cloth; sometimes this makes the weft invisible, which is useful for weaving a dense cloth, perhaps for a hardwearing belt. For a weft-faced weave, the warp is spaced more loosely and there are more p.p.i. than e.p.i. This is the case in traditional tapestry weaving, in which the warp is hidden.

TWILL

Twill is the simplest weave structure after plain weave. It is another traditional weave, which has an older name, "tweel." This is thought to have come from the French word, *touaille*. Twill is the most flexible of woven structures and so is frequently used in fashion fabrics.

The pliable nature of twill is due to there being fewer intersections of warp and weft. Its defining characteristic is a climbing diagonal line that is made up of weft or warp floats. In a balanced twill, as illustrated in the chart below, the weft travels over two warp threads, under the next two warp threads, and this pattern is then repeated across the pick. On the following pick, the float over two warps shifts one thread in the direction of the diagonal. This shift continues from one pick to the next, so building up the diagonal line. The ratio of warp and weft can be varied, thus altering the balance of the twill, while the structure remains the same. A balanced twill (2/2, shown in the chart and the samples opposite) creates a 45-degree diagonal. In a 3/1 twill, the weft passes under three warp threads and over one warp thread. This makes the warp dominant and creates a larger angle. Conversely, in a 1/3 twill, the weft passes under one warp thread and over three. This creates a weft-faced cloth with a tighter angle.

There is so much to say about twills and their weave variations—this is merely the beginning! Herringbone weave and traditional bird's eye are two examples of such variations and are described in more detail later in this section (see pages 78-79 and 84-85, respectively).

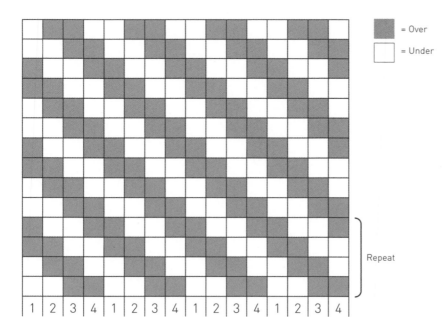

■ = Over

□ = Under

Repeat

1 2 3 4 1 2 3 4 1 2 3 4 1 2 3 4

WEAVE CHART

This should be read from bottom to top, right to left. After the fourth line, the pattern repeats.

FIXING FLOATS ON SELVAGES

The sequence of the lifted warp threads in a twill pattern will always leave long floats on the warp selvages, where the last warps do not catch. If you notice this happening, tuck the shuttle over or under that particular warp thread in order to draw it back into the woven cloth.

HERRINGBONE WEAVE

Herringbone weave, with its distinctive zigzag pattern, is familiar to most people. It is a traditional weave structure that is often found in menswear fashion fabrics and tweeds. Herringbone is a variation of the twill structure and is sometimes referred to as "pointed twill." The diagonal line of the twill is mirrored to create a horizontal zigzag or chevron shape. This is made by reversing the pick-up sequence of the warp threads at a certain point and repeating across the row. Countless adaptations of this structure have been developed over centuries by many weavers. Here, I have outlined the herringbone weave in its simplest form.

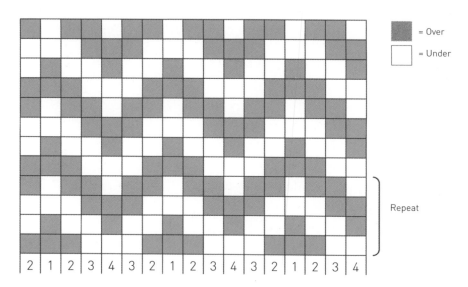

= Over

= Under

Repeat

2 1 2 3 4 3 2 1 2 3 4 3 2 1 2 3 4

WEAVE CHART

This should be read from bottom to top, right to left. After the fourth line, the pattern repeats.

I love the idea that the skeleton of the herring fish is the namesake of this pattern. It conjures up images of coastal communities of weavers and fishermen, possibly in the West of Scotland.

BASKET WEAVE

Basket weave is also sometimes known as "hopsack." While the weaving process is very similar to that of plain weave, basket weave has a very different texture. It creates a strong, textured, checkered pattern made up of large blocks. Structurally, basket weave consists of grouping the warp and weft threads to extend the plain weave both vertically and horizontally. Two adjacent warp threads are grouped and act in the same manner, as do two weft picks. This happens by repeating the same shed, which, as you will notice, can cause some problems. For example, it is easy to undo a pick that you have just completed, unless you tuck the weft around the first warp on the second pick of each shed. This will catch the weft so that it stays in place. In general, in basket weave, the threads are grouped in sets of two, but this can be varied to alter the scale of the blocks. Why not try grouping four threads? Be careful, though: the larger the blocks, the fewer intersections of warp and weft there will be, making the cloth less stable.

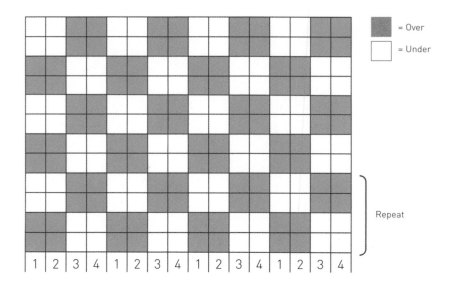

= Over

= Under

Repeat

1 2 3 4 1 2 3 4 1 2 3 4 1 2 3 4

WEAVE CHART

This should be read from bottom to top, right to left.
After the fourth line, the pattern repeats.

Early on in my weaving journey, I dismissed basket weave as being too simple. It is only recently that I have come back to it and discovered its diversity. Varying the scale of the blocks and combining basket weave with plain weave across one pick can have interesting results. Another idea to consider, when you're feeling a bit more confident, is to weave with two shuttles of different yarns, weaving one pick of plain weave between each basket-weave pick. The result is called an "overshot" pattern, which can have really exciting color mixes!

RIB

Rib weave is another simple weave structure with a striking texture. It consists of alternate weaving two picks, which are the opposite of each other and where there are long weft floats. The floats on each side of the cloth are repeated over the same warp threads in subsequent picks. This creates a rib effect, forming vertical columns of raised ridges across the warp as the weft floats stack up on top of each other. Weaving on opposites means that, in every pick, the weft travels over every warp thread it passed under in the previous pick, and vice versa. In rib weave, this is repeated with just two sheds for the entire pattern. This makes for a very strong, dense cloth in which the weft packs down tightly, often covering the warp.

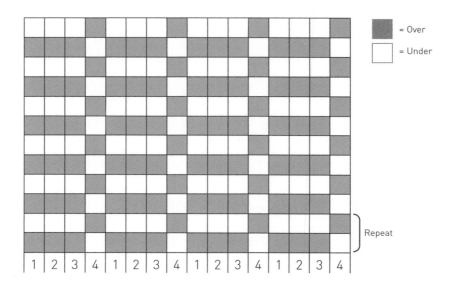

■ = Over

□ = Under

Repeat

| 1 | 2 | 3 | 4 | 1 | 2 | 3 | 4 | 1 | 2 | 3 | 4 | 1 | 2 | 3 | 4 |

WEAVE CHART

This should be read from bottom to top, right to left. After the second line, the pattern repeats.

To truly show off this weave structure, you must weave it in two contrasting colors with two shuttles. Whichever color you choose to be dominant, weave this color on the picks with weft floats on the right side of the cloth. This technique can be seen in the project for the Placemat (see pages 118–121).

TRADITIONAL BIRD'S EYE

Traditional bird's eye is another traditional weave and also part of the twill family. It is a variation of herringbone weave in which the progression of picks is reflected back on itself. Here, I have given an example of bird's eye weave in its simplest form, as a repeat over six threads.

Since bird's eye is a traditional weave structure, endless variations exist, as well as many different names. For example, it is sometimes referred to as "pointed twill" or "goose eye." The zigzags of herringbone weave are reversed to form diamonds with a dot or "eye" in the center. The eye can become more pronounced through the use of color (see the project for the *Placemat*, pages 118–121). To achieve the most striking diamond, use a heavier weft yarn in a strong contrasting color to the warp. This will make the warp threads more visible and give a defined outline to the diamond. Similarly, the scale of the diamond can be enlarged by increasing the number of warp threads in the repeat.

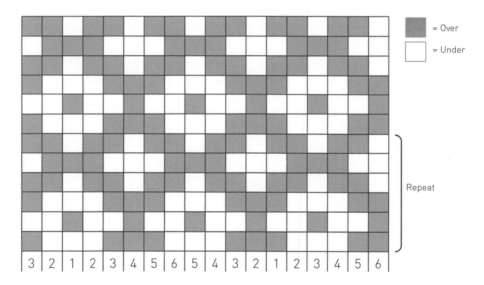

■ = Over

□ = Under

Repeat

3 2 1 2 3 4 5 6 5 4 3 2 1 2 3 4 5 6

WEAVE CHART

This should be read from bottom to top, right to left. After the sixth line, the pattern repeats.

If you would like to experiment further with the bird's eye weave structure, have a go at drawing out your desired diamonds on graph paper in a similar way to the charts that feature in this section. The shaded squares will be where the weft passes over the warp.

EDGING TECHNIQUES

———

This section looks at what to do once you have come to the end of your weaving and are ready to add some finishing touches.

———

When you are nearing the end of your work, you will notice that the warp tension changes, becoming either far too slack or too tight. It will become difficult to create a shed to pass the shuttle through, as there will be no gap between the two sets of threads. When this occurs, you have come to the end of your weaving. Equally, you may have reached the end of a weaving project or woven a sufficient amount and decided to finish before the challenge of warp tension occurs.

Essentially, to take your weaving off the frame loom, the warp threads are cut horizontally across the top and bottom of the weaving. However, before you grab the scissors and become snip-happy, there are a few things to consider. As the warp threads are dressed on the loom, they are stretched under tension. As soon as they are cut, they will slacken and shrink a little, so it is very possible that the first and last few weft picks will come undone. There are several methods, or edging techniques, that you can use to prevent this from happening.

The main aim of edging techniques is to secure your weaving along any open edges to prevent it from fraying. It is also an opportunity to add decorative detail to the piece. There are several ways of doing this. Some are more decorative than others, while others are more suitable for specific items, depending on the piece you have woven. In the next few pages, I outline some of my favorite edging techniques—machine zigzag, hemstitching, fringing, knot and darn edging, and hanging through warp loops, as well as how to make tassels. Some of these finishes are carried out before the weaving is cut from the loom, while others are completed afterward.

MACHINE ZIGZAG

Machine zigzag is a stitched edging technique. It is a quick and useful edging technique if you have access to a sewing machine. Machine zigzag secures the warp and weft together through stitching.

1 Before taking your piece off the loom, weave a few picks of scrap yarn as a header, which can be taken out later. This will prevent the last picks from unraveling.

2 Cut the warp threads horizontally across the top and bottom, about ½ in. (1 cm) from the weaving.

3 Sew a line of zigzag stitch across the first pick of weft, ensuring you catch the warp and weft threads.

4 Repeat Step 3 across the last pick of weft.

5 Trim the excess warp tails close to the lines of zigzagged stitching.

To neaten the edging further, you might wish to fold the edge and sew it into a rolled hem with a line of straight stitch.

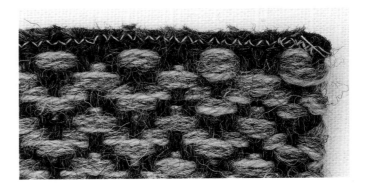

HEMSTITCHING

Hemstitching is my favorite edging technique for frame-loom weaving (and for floor-loom weaving, for that matter). This is a very traditional technique and avoids the need to use a sewing machine. It can be sewn in the same yarn as the weft yarn to leave a nearly invisible finish. Hemstitching secures the warp and weft together through stitching. It is an excellent technique for adding fringing, without having to tie 20 or more knots across the warp. It is sewn when the piece of weaving it still in tension on the loom.

YOU WILL NEED

Bodkin/darning needle

Scissors

Weft yarn or similar thread of choice (about three times the length of the warp width)

1   Reverse side

1 Thread the needle with sufficient yarn (you'll need about three times the length of the warp width). Beginning on the reverse side of the weaving, sew a double stitch into the selvage to secure the end.

2 Working from the front side of the weaving, pass the needle under the first two warp ends at the right-hand selvage, moving from right to left. Pull the needle through completely with the yarn following.

3 Pass the thread back over these two warp threads, from left to right. Bring the needle from the reverse side through to the front, surfacing beyond the two warp threads that you just wrapped. Stitch in, two weft shots deep. Try to catch a warp thread too, to make the stitch more secure.

4 Pull the yarn tight so that the warp threads are pulled together to form a fringe.

5 Repeat Steps 2–4, to create more fringes, until you reach the left-hand selvage.

2   Front side

__3__   Front side

__4__   Front side

__5__   Front side

__6__   Reverse side

__7__

6 To secure at the left-hand selvage, sew another double stitch on the reverse side of the weaving, as before. To tuck the tail, thread the needle through a few stitches on the reverse. Trim the yarn here.

7 After cutting and pulling out the heading cord, repeat the process across the beginning of the piece of weaving. When you have finished hemstitching both ends, cut the warp threads as far away from the weaving as possible. Then trim the fringe to the desired length.

FRINGING

Fringing is an edging technique that takes place as you cut the weaving off the frame loom. It calls for some advance planning, if you would like fringing of an equal length on both edges of your piece. To allow for longer fringing, at the beginning of your piece, start the heading cords as high as required to leave longer "empty" warp threads. Usually, on a frame loom, about 2 in. (5 cm) of fringing can be achieved with the heading cord in the usual position (i.e. roughly ½ in./1.5 cm above the base bar). This differs from frame loom to frame loom, though, so do measure if you have a required length in mind. Fringing makes a nice edging for a placemat. The number of ends you choose to group together for your fringe depends on the sett, yarn thickness, and personal preference! For a finer fringe, choose fewer; for a bulkier fringe, choose more! In this sample, I have grouped two threads together.

YOU WILL NEED

Bodkin/darning needle
Scissors

1 Cut the warp ends at the bottom of the frame loom, as close to the bottom bar as possible (a). Only cut about a quarter of the ends (b).

2 Tie a group of warp ends together using an Overhand Knot (see *Knots*, page 97). To do this, make a loop close to the edge of the weaving (a) and pull the ends through the loop (b). Here, I grouped two threads together. With a finer yarn, you can group more threads together.

3 Tighten so that the knot sits close to the fell of the weaving.

4 Continue cutting and tying off the ends in groups until you reach the other selvage.

5 Repeat the process across the top of the weaving for a fringe on both sides of the piece.

6 Once all the knots have been tied, trim the fringing to the desired length with a straight cut.

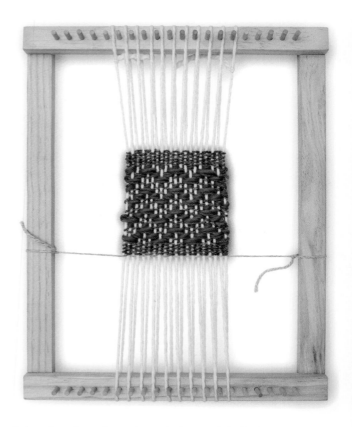

A piece of weaving under tension on the loom ready for fringing.

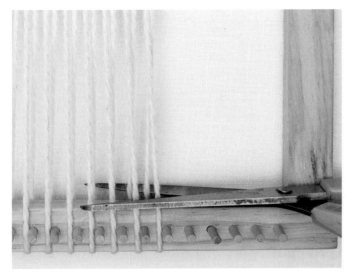

1a

1b

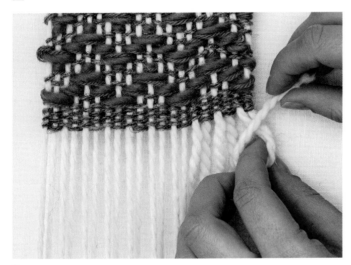

2a

2b

3

6

KNOT AND DARN EDGING

I really like this edging technique because it is quite clean and flat. It does not lose any length in the woven piece, while also not adding any additional bulk. This technique is applied once the weaving has been removed from the loom.

YOU WILL NEED

Bodkin/darning needle
Scissors

1 After cutting the warp threads to leave a long fringe and taking the weaving off the loom, lay the piece flat, with the reverse side facing up. Beginning at the right-hand selvage, take the first two warp threads, A and B. Wrap the right-hand warp thread, A, over and underneath the left-hand warp end, B, bringing thread A back up through the loop it just formed. Pull up tight to the weaving.

2 Taking the next warp end, C, repeat the same technique with warp end B (replacing A with B and B with C).

3 Continue working in this way, from right to left, across the entire warp.

4 Thread the first warp end through the bodkin or darning needle. For an invisible finish, darn the needle down through the weaving, following the pattern and path of that particular warp thread for about 1 in. (2.5 cm). Pull the needle all the way through.

5 Continue threading the needle and darning each warp end in this way, following its individual path (a). Keep darning across the warp until you reach the other side of the piece (b).

6 When all the warp ends have been darned, trim the tails close to the weaving.

1

2

3

4

5a

5b

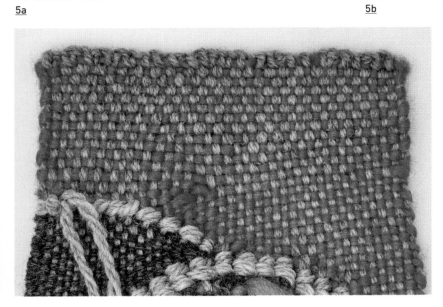

6

HANGING THROUGH WARP LOOPS

This edging is popular for woven wall-hanging pieces. Using foraged driftwood, rather than a plain rod/dowel, will turn your work into a real statement piece. The method is used for the *Woven Wall Hanging* (see pages 102–107). If you wish, you can even paint the rod/dowel to match the colors of the weaving. As with hemstitching, this edging is applied while the weaving is still in the loom.

YOU WILL NEED

Rod/dowel or a piece of foraged driftwood (this must be longer than the warp width)
Scissors
Hanging thread or line

1 Insert the rod into the natural shed, so that it is lying close to the fell of the weaving.

2 Cut the lower set of warp threads, about halfway between the fell of the weaving and the top bar of the frame. As the warp ends are attached to each other, this will also cut the higher set of warp threads. You should now have fringing of two lengths, alternating at every thread (i.e. one long, one short). The long threads will be draping over the rod, while the short threads lie underneath.

3 Beginning at the right-hand selvage, tie together a pair of adjacent long and short warp ends. Tie in a Square Knot (see *Knots*, page 97), so that the knot is sitting on the reverse of the rod and is not visible from the front. Tie in a loose single knot. Continue working from right to left until all the pairs of warp threads have been tied.

4 Flip the piece over, so that the reverse side is facing up. Tighten all the knots, pushing the rod down to the fell of the weaving (a). Tie the ends of the threads in secure double knots across the warp. Trim any long tails (b).

5 Now you can tie a hanging thread or line to either end of the rod and your piece is ready for hanging up and putting on display!

1

2

3

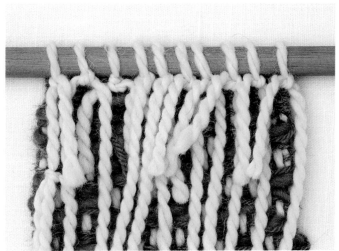

4a

4b

5

TASSELS

Tassels add a decorative hanging detail. They can either be used as a fringe made after the piece comes off the loom, or within the weaving itself and stitched in as surface decoration. A tassel also makes a great zipper pull, as in the *Foldover Purse* (see pages 108-117). You can use a variety of yarns to add texture and color.

YOU WILL NEED

Tape measure
Scissors
Yarn

1 Measure multiple lengths of yarn, twice the desired length of your tassel. The number of strands in the tassel will depend on how dense you would like the tassel to be. In this example, I used about 15 strands of 10-ply yarn, each approximately 12 in. (30 cm) long. Set aside two extra lengths for the hanging loop and the tying strand.

2 Fold the multistranded bundle of yarn lengths in half. Pass the hanging-loop strand through the fold, then tie in an Overhand Knot (see *Knots*, page 97).

3 Twist the knotted hanging loop round so that the knot is tucked under the fold. Lay the tying strand underneath the bundle, about ¾ in. (2 cm) from the top of the fold.

4 Tie the ends of the tying strand together in a Square Knot (see *Knots*, page 97), pulling it tightly around the folded bundle of yarns to gather the ends and form the head of the tassel. Let the tails hang down to form lots of strands.

5 Trim the strands to the desired length and suspend your tassel from the hanging loop.

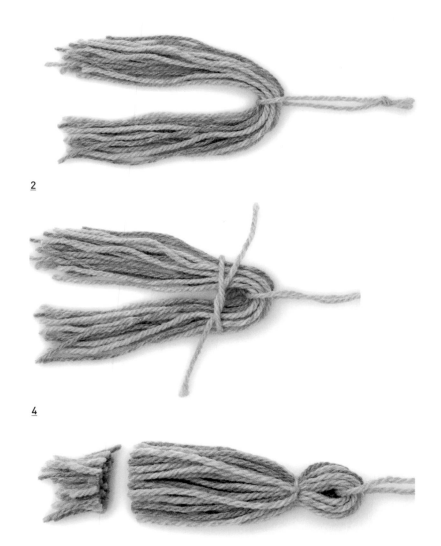

KNOTS

The following four knots are used in various techniques and projects throughout the book.

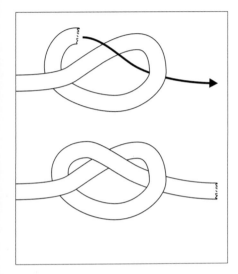

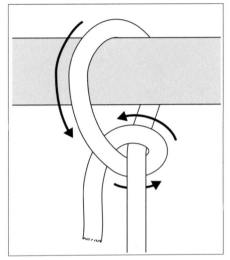

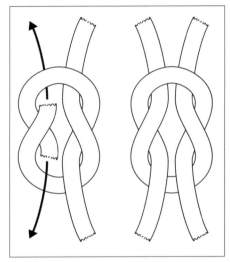

OVERHAND KNOT

1 Take the tail end of the thread under, then over itself, sliding it through the loop you just created.

2 Pull both ends of the thread in opposite directions to tighten.

HALF HITCH KNOT

1 Wrap the thread around the object once. You now have two ends of thread—the active thread on the left and the center thread on the right. Thread the active thread under the center thread from the right and up through the opening on the left.

2 Pull the active thread tight to complete the knot.

SQUARE KNOT

1 Start with two pieces of yarn. Lay the left thread over the right, then pass it under the right thread and up through the opening between them. Pull both threads evenly in opposite directions to tighten.

2 The second half is a reverse of the first half. Lay the right thread over the left, then pass it under the left thread and up through the opening between them. Pull both threads equally in opposite directions to tighten the knot.

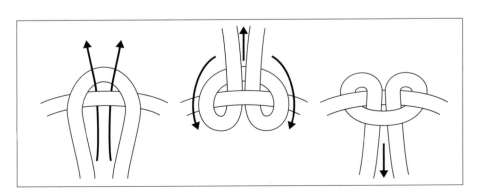

LARK'S HEAD KNOT

1 Start by folding the knotting thread in half to form a loop, then pass the loop under the other thread (the base thread).

2 Take both tail ends of the knotting thread over the base thread and through the loop.

3 Tighten.

FINISHING TECHNIQUES:
FROM WEAVING TO CLOTH

———

Finishing techniques are those processes that a piece of weaving undergoes after edging. Although the techniques are done by hand, they will bring your woven piece to a higher standard and give it a professional feel. Similar to knitting, a piece of weaving is not finished until it has been washed and fulled. This gives the fibers a chance to settle in and get cozy with the fibers in the yarns next to them, helping to fix them in their permanent home. This process is called fulling. Essentially, it stabilizes the cloth and is also a great opportunity for any mishaps to "disappear."

———

Loom-state weaving is the term used to describe weaving straight off the loom. It is two sets of threads woven together, but not yet transformed into cloth or "finished." For fibers to come together and full, a few elements are necessary; moisture, soap, and friction. A careful and cautious measure of each is wise! The purpose of washing is not to clean the weaving, but to full it, although the cleanliness is a nice added bonus.

As we know, yarns are made of different types of fiber. They therefore differ in how they act in the finishing processes and need to be handled slightly differently. As a general rule, taking the fibers used in the projects in this book, we can group cotton and linen together as plant fibers and place wool in a separate category of animal fibers. Furthermore, how you approach the finishing stage will depend on how

you have woven the fiber and subsequently how you wash it. This will always differ from person to person, so do keep note of how you finish particular yarns so that you can replicate the process subsequently. To learn more about a particular fiber and how it acts, read through *Meet the Materials* (see pages 22–27).

In general, to finish weaving, loom-state weaving goes through a series of the following processes: washing, drying (and sometimes blocking), and pressing. I have provided some guidelines on these processes here. So much more could be written about the different finishing techniques—this is merely a starting point! My main advice is to experiment and keep good records until you discover the finished effect you like when using a particular yarn.

ANIMAL FIBER TYPES: WOOL

Wool will shrink in the washing process by approximately 5–10 percent, depending on the yarn, the weave structure, the water temperature, etc., and also the way you handle it. When you are washing wool or any other animal fiber, always wash in tepid water with sparing amounts of soap. Always rinse with cold water.

PLANT FIBER TYPES: COTTON AND LINEN

Cotton and linen can handle warmer water temperatures than wool—and even benefit from it! For plant fibers, I use slightly hotter water than listed in instructions. Rinse in cool water.

HANDWASHING

Half-fill a container with lukewarm/tepid water. Add a few soap flakes or a dash of washing detergent and mix through the water. Fully dunk the piece of weaving into the water so that it is completely saturated. Slowly swirl the piece around in the water. Gently squeeze and release the piece repeatedly to create a gentle agitation, continuously moving it about. Continue for five minutes. Leave the piece to soak for up to an hour. Drain and then rinse the piece of weaving in cold water until the water runs clear. Squeeze out the excess water. Do not wring or twist, as this will distort the shape.

DRYING

In the drying process, I treat animal and plant fibers in a similar way.

Leave the piece of weaving to dry flat. Place the piece on a flat towel in a warm environment to air-dry naturally. Do not leave in direct sunlight.

SLOW SPIN

Another method for getting rid of excess water after rinsing a piece of weaving is to use a slow spin cycle on your washing machine. I would only recommend doing this for larger pieces, or if you are washing multiple pieces together. You will need to experiment with your machine's settings to find a suitable spin. Bear in mind that further shrinkage may occur during spinning. This can be a great addition to the fulling process, but be careful not to do it for too long or the piece will felt.

BLOCKING

Blocking is not essential for all woven pieces, but can be done as part of the drying process. Blocking means to stretch a fabric while it is wet and then hold it in place until it dries.

Lay the wet piece flat on a board and pin it into the desired stretched shape. Make sure to align the piece so that the warp and weft are perpendicular to each other. Leave to dry in a warm environment, away from direct sunlight.

PRESSING

To further improve the finish of your weaving once it has dried, you can press it with a domestic steam iron. This is another opportunity to flatten and shape the piece. You may decide to do this instead of, or in addition to, blocking.

For animal-fiber types, set the iron to a low heat/wool setting with the steam on. Pull the piece into the desired shape as you press. The steam from the iron adds moisture to the fibers again and makes them flexible, allowing you to further manipulate them if necessary.

To avoid a shiny finish on your woolen cloth, place a towel over the woolen piece while you are pressing it.

For plant-fiber types, follow the instructions given for animal-fiber types, but adjust the temperature setting to a high heat or the cotton/linen setting on your iron.

CHAPTER 3

THE PROJECTS

WOVEN WALL HANGING

——

This project is inspired by the recent trend for woven wall hangings and uses a combination of the rug-making and tapestry techniques outlined earlier in the book. The layered rya knots create tiers of colored fringing, which is a simple way to add length to a piece. Made with natural wool, a woven wall hanging is perfect for displaying in your home to add a bit of coziness! This piece of weaving involves no further construction once it has been woven, and is ready to be displayed straight from the loom.

——

TOOLS

Frame loom
Stick shuttle
Shed stick
Scissors
Beater/fork
Postcard (optional)

MATERIALS

Makes 1 wall hanging
Warp:
Yarn A 1 x ¾-oz (50-g) ball of Drops Alaska Dark Gray 05
Weft:
Yarn B 2 x 3½-oz (100-g) balls of Drops Andes Dark Gray 0519
Yarn C 1 x ¾-oz (50-g) ball of Drops Eskimo Yellow 24
Yarn D 1 x ¾-oz (50-g) ball of Drops Eskimo Medium Gray 46
Yarn E 1 x ¾-oz (50-g) ball of Drops Eskimo Camel 13
Yarn F 1 x 3½-oz (100-g) ball of Drops Andes Beige 0619
Yarn G 2 x ¾-oz (50-g) balls of Drops Alaska Mustard 58

DRESSING THE LOOM: SPEC DETAILS

Sett: 4 ends per inch (2.5 cm)
Warp width: 8 in. (20 cm)
Total warp ends: 32
Beat: 10 picks per inch (2.5 cm)

To dress the loom, wind the warp yarn, Yarn A, using the figure-eight method (see page 36). Wind from the top left-hand corner to the right. Space the warp so that, from the front, one thread is wound in each dent, giving an overall sett of four threads per inch (2.5 cm). Finish dressing the loom with a heading cord (see *Setting Up The Frame Loom*, pages 38–40).

Skill level: Easy
Dimensions: 16 x 8 in. (40 x 20 cm)

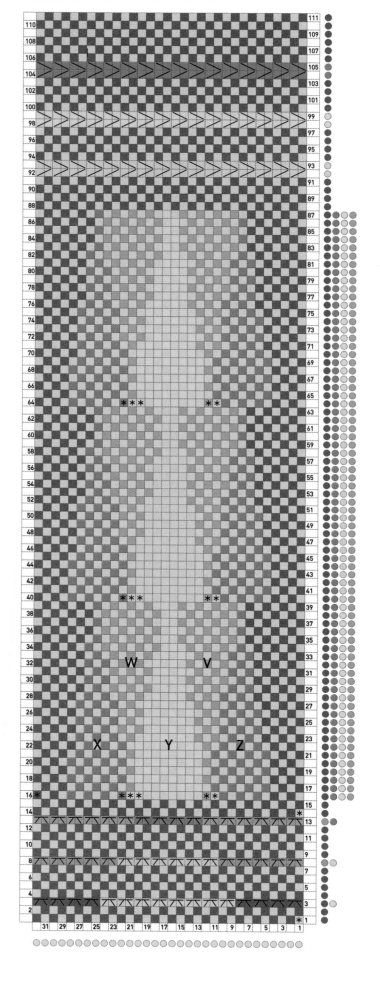

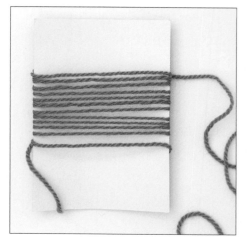

Use a piece of card to measure out the strands of yarn used for the rya knots in Steps 2 and 3.

▢ = Yarn A

■ = Yarn B

▢ = Yarn C

▢ = Yarn D

▢ = Yarn E

▢ = Yarn F

▢ = Yarn G

＊ = Begin weft here

◹ = Soumak stitch

◸ = Soumak stitch

⊼ = Rya knot

All woven in PLAIN WEAVE, unless Rya Knot or Soumak Stitch as indicated

1

2

1 Begin by weaving two picks of plain weave (see pages 74–75) in Yarn B, starting from the right-hand selvage. Leave the shuttle attached. For the first row of rya-knot fringing, cut lengths of Yarns B and C using the height of the loom as a guide (about 16 in./40 cm). As each rya knot is tied with two strands of yarn worked over two warp threads, you will need 16 strands each of Yarns B and C. Starting at the left-hand selvage, tie four rya knots (see pages 66–67) in Yarn B, eight rya knots in Yarn C, and four rya knots in Yarn B. All warp threads should now be used.

2 Weave four picks of plain weave in Yarn B. For the second row of rya knots, cut 20 strands of Yarn D and 12 strands of Yarn E. Use a postcard as a template, if you wish, wrapping the yarn lengthwise around the postcard, held portrait. Cut the yarn at the base of the card only, to give an approximate length of 12 in. (30 cm). Again, using two strands per knot and working from left to right, tie five rya knots in Yarn D, six knots in Yarn E, and five knots in Yarn D.

3 Weave four picks of plain weave in Yarn B. For the third row of rya knots, cut 24 strands of Yarn F and 16 strands of Yarn G. Wrap the yarn around the postcard, but this time wrap it landscape. Cut the yarn at one side of the postcard only, giving an approximate length of 8¾ in. (22 cm). Working from left to right, tie six rya knots in Yarn F using two strands per knot. For the center, using Yarn G, tie four knots with four strands per knot. Finish the fringing with six knots in Yarn F. Weave two picks of plain weave in Yarn B.

3

4 To weave the triangle pattern section, multiple wefts are used. Wind two finger skeins of Yarns F, G, and B, plus one finger skein each of Yarns C and E. For the first row of triangles, begin by weaving the triangle shapes—following the instructions for weaving triangles on pages 58–60—then weave up the background sections. Using Yarn G, weave triangle X, as per the chart, over seven warp threads at its base (warp threads 5–11). Skip one warp thread and, using Yarn C, weave triangle Y, as per the chart, worked over eight warp threads at its base (warp threads 13–20). Skip one warp thread and, using the second finger skein of Yarn G, weave triangle Z, as per the chart. Weave the dark gray background sections on either side of the first row of triangles with the finger skeins of Yarn B, as per the chart, up to the same pick as the triangles.

TIP When you are weaving with multiple wefts in the triangles section, push any finger skeins that are not in use to the reverse side of the weaving. That way, you can easily start weaving with each one again without having a large float across the front of the wall hanging.

5 To weave the background triangle W, use a Half Hitch Knot (see *Knots*, page 97) to attach a finger skein of Yarn F to the single warp thread between triangles X and Y (i.e. warp thread 12, as per the chart) in the same way that you finished the points of the first three triangles in the row. To weave background triangle V, use another Half Hitch Knot to attach the second finger skein of Yarn F to the single warp thread between triangles Y and Z (i.e. warp thread 21, as per the chart). Weave triangles W and V, leaving no warp threads empty between the triangles.

6 Continue weaving rows two and three of the triangles, as per the instructions in Steps 4 and 5, and following the chart. The same finger skeins can be continued from the first row in all cases except for triangle Y. For this triangle, cut off the finger skein of Yarn C on the reverse side. Then, for the second triangle row, weave triangle Y in Yarn E. For the last triangle row, weave triangle Y in Yarn C again, as per the chart. Once the three rows of triangles are complete, weave two picks of plain weave with the Yarn B shuttle.

7 With a finger skein of Yarn E, weave one braid of Soumak Stitch (see pages 68–69) from the right-hand selvage to the left-hand selvage. Weave four more picks of Yarn B.

8 Repeat Step 7, using a finger skein of Yarn C for the second soumak braid. Repeat once more with a finger skein of double-stranded Yarn G for the third soumak braid. After weaving a further six picks of plain weave in Yarn B, cut and tuck the weft tail.

9 To remove your wall hanging from the loom, follow the method for *Hanging through Warp Loops* (see pages 94–95) across the top. To finish the bottom of the wall hanging, follow the technique for *Fringing* (see pages 90–91). Make sure to cut the warp threads at the very base of the frame loom to tie the fringing.

4–5

6

7

8

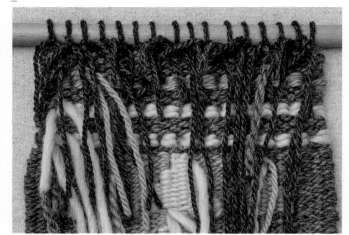

9 BACK

9 FRONT

FOLDOVER PURSE

———

This purse project consists of a two-color warp, alternating on every thread—known as a "1–1 warp." It is a very effective way of introducing more color variation to a project. It also makes clever use of the natural shed to create basket weave. This piece features a decorative tassel on the zipper pull, which turns it into a very stylish purse or makeup bag!

———

TOOLS

Frame loom
Stick shuttle
Shed stick
Scissors
Beater/fork
Sewing machine
Sewing machine thread
Sewing pins
Iron
8-in. (20-cm) brass zipper
8½ x 10-in. (21.5 x 25-cm) piece of cotton lining fabric
Sewing needle and thread

MATERIALS

Makes 1 purse
Warp:
Yarn A 1 x ¾-oz (50-g) ball of Drops Bomull-Lin Gray Blue 20
Yarn B 1 x ¾-oz (50-g) ball of Drops Bomull-Lin Beige 11
Weft:
Yarn C 2 x ¾-oz (50-g) balls of Drops Bomull-Lin Dark Blue 21
Yarn D 1 x ¾-oz (50-g) ball of Drops Belle Cotton Dandelion 04
Yarn E 1 x ¾-oz (50-g) ball of Drops Bomull-Lin Beige 11

DRESSING THE LOOM: SPEC DETAILS

Sett: 8 ends per inch (2.5 cm)
Warp width: 8½ in. (21.5 cm)
Total warp ends: 68
Beat: 14 picks per inch (2.5 cm)—single stranded—and 10 picks per inch (2.5 cm)—double-stranded

For this project the loom is dressed slightly differently. Although still dressed using the figure-eight method (see page 36), this time two yarns are wound together simultaneously. This creates a 1–1 warp in which, across the warp, every thread alternates between Yarn A and Yarn B. Dressing the loom in this way introduces more color variation to a piece. See overleaf for instructions on how to do this.

Skill level: Easy
Dimensions: 4½ x 6¾ in. (11 x 17 cm)

1

2

1 Tie the two warp yarns, Yarns A and B, together around the top bar of the loom in the second dent from the left-hand side. Hold your index finger between the two warp yarns and bring it downward.

2 Wind the two warp yarns using the figure-eight method (see page 36). Keep your index finger in between Yarns A and B as you wind. This will stop the yarns from becoming tangled and also ensure that the correct order of the warp threads—ABABABABAB, etc.—is maintained. Space the warp so that from the front of the loom two threads are wound in each dent, giving an overall sett of 8 threads per inch (2.5 cm).

3 Continue winding in this way until you reach the second last dent on the right-hand side of the loom and 68 warp threads have been wound. Cut and tie off Yarns A and B together around the top bar. Finish dressing the loom with a heading cord (see pages 38–40).

3

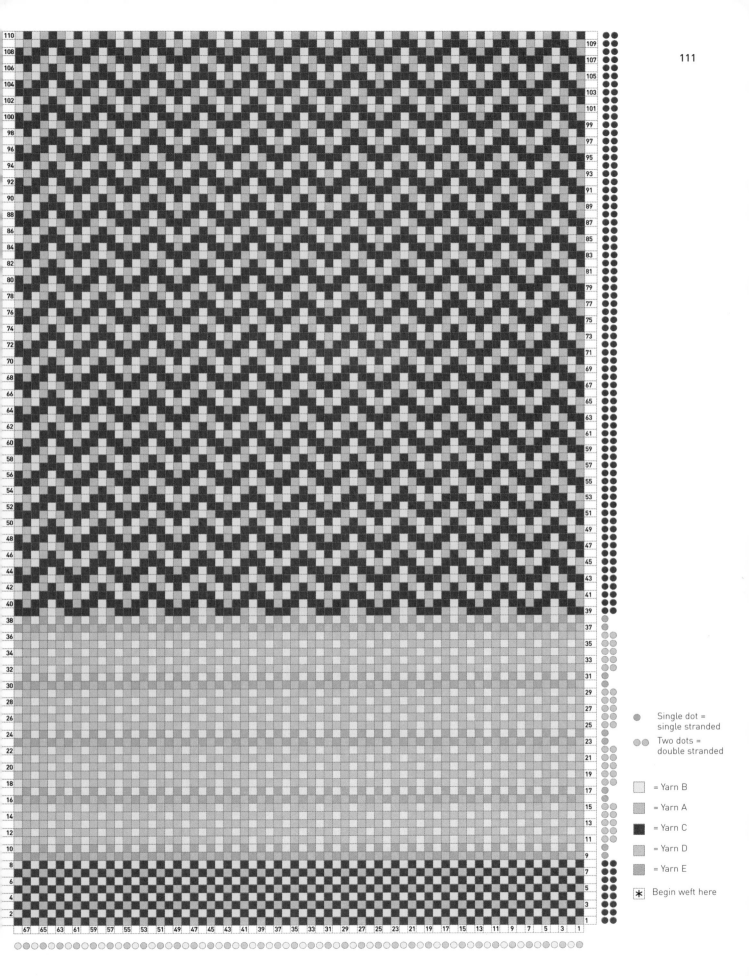

Single dot =
single stranded

Two dots =
double stranded

= Yarn B

= Yarn A

= Yarn C

= Yarn D

= Yarn E

✳ Begin weft here

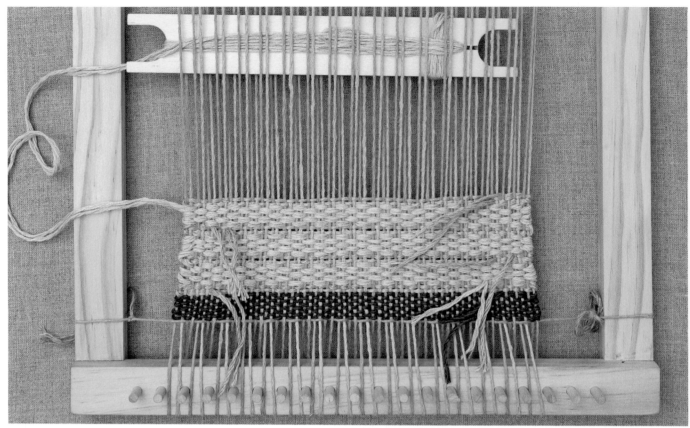

4

4 Weave the weft using Yarns C, D, and E, following the chart. When weaving the basket weave (see pages 80–81) with Yarn D, the weft is double-stranded. Wind two strands of Yarn D together onto a stick shuttle. Weave as if the strands were one weft. You can use the natural shed created by the 1-1 warp when weaving basket weave.

5 To weave the main body of the purse with herringbone weave (see pages 78–79), the weft is also double-stranded with Yarn C. Wind the shuttle as described in Step 4. Weave following the chart.

6 Continue weaving in herringbone until you finish the chart or the piece reaches a length of approximately 10 in. (25 cm) on the loom. To edge, either hemstitch (see pages 88–89) on the loom or cut the piece from the loom and machine zigzag (see page 87). Once the piece is edged and removed from the loom, finish the cloth (see *Finishing Techniques: From Weaving to Cloth*, pages 98–99).

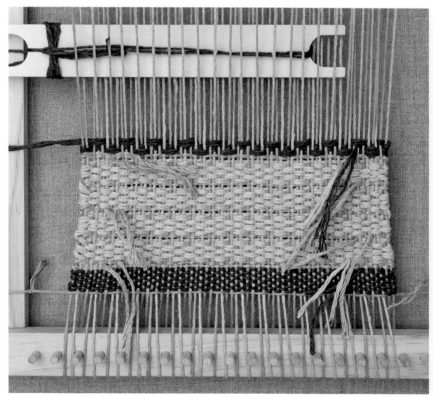

5

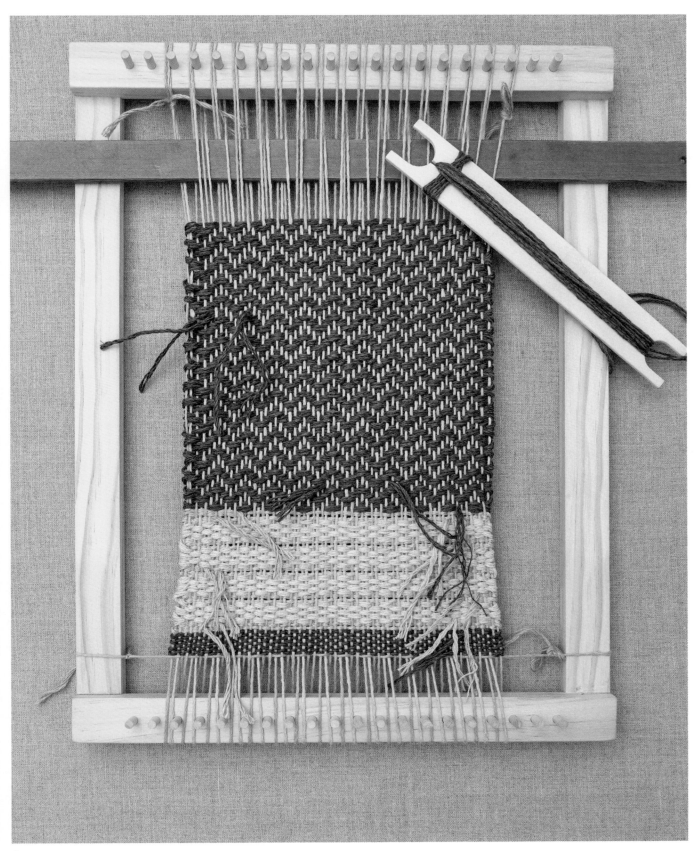

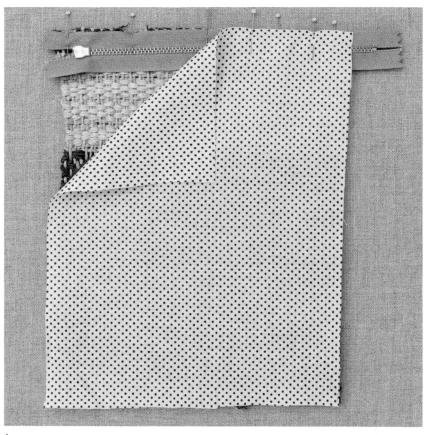

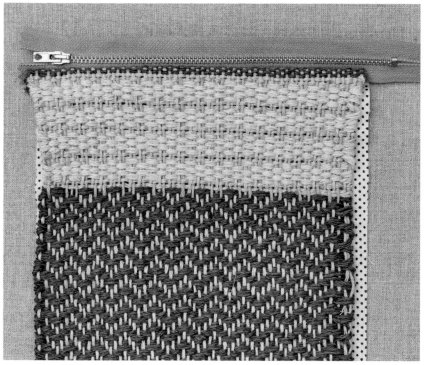

1

2

PURSE CONSTRUCTION

1 To construct the lined purse, you'll need to fit the zipper first. To do this, lay the zipper on top of the woven cloth, with right sides facing. Pin the zipper in place. Lay the lining fabric on top, face to face, sandwiching the zipper between the two layers. Pin in place. Using a zipper foot on your sewing machine, sew the layers together, close to the zipper coils.

2 Press the seam open and trim any loose threads. Turn the lining over the zipper and match the reverse side of the woven cloth to the reverse side of the lining.

3 Fold the woven cloth over, face to face, and line it up with the other edge of the zipper. Pin in place. Turn the purse over. Fold the lining fabric over, face to face, and line it up with the zipper edge. Pin in place. This will sandwich the zipper once more between the lining and the woven cloth. Using a zipper foot on your sewing machine, sew the layers together, close to the zipper coils as before. Press the seam and trim any loose threads.

4 Lay the purse flat with the zipper in the center. Pin the edges of the woven cloth and the lining on three sides, as shown. Open the zipper halfway. Using the normal foot on your sewing machine, sew all three sides, as pinned. Press the seams and trim any loose threads.

5 Turn the purse the right way out by opening the zipper and pulling through the unsewn side of the lining. Pin the lining and handstitch the open side. Push the sewn lining back inside the woven outer purse. To make a decorative tassel for the zipper pull, follow the instructions on *Tassels* (see page 96).

Yarns for the tassel: Use Yarns A and B to make the body of the tassel and Yarn D for the tying strand. Attach the finished tassel to the zipper pull using a hanging loop in Yarn A.

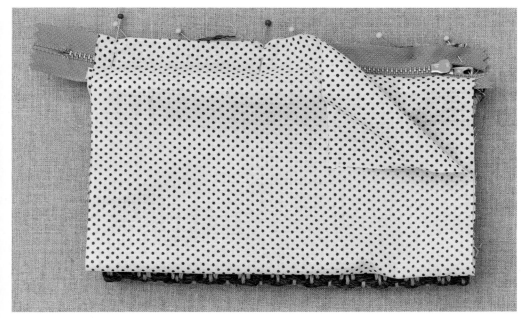

3

4

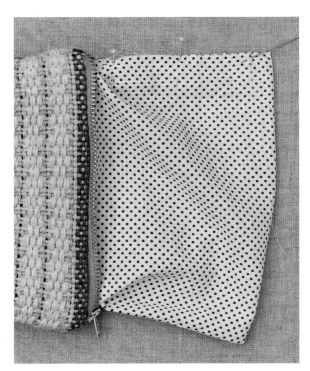

5

PLACEMAT

———

The materials used for this placemat are the natural fibers of linen and cotton. These lend themselves perfectly to tableware, since they are easy to clean. This project incorporates many of the weave structures outlined earlier in the book, including plain weave, rib, twill, and traditional bird's eye. You can repeat the pattern to make a set of four or more placemats, or mix and match the structures to create your own patterns!

———

TOOLS

Frame loom
2 shuttles
Shed stick
Scissors
Beater/fork

MATERIALS

Warp:

Yarn A 1 x ¾-oz (50-g) ball of Drops Heart You Navy Blue 05

Yarn B 1 x ¾-oz (50-g) ball of Drops Heart You Coral 109

Weft:

Yarn C 1 x ¾-oz (50-g) ball of Drops Heart You Coral 109

Yarn D 1 x ¾-oz (50-g) ball of Drops Bomull-Lin Brown 05

Yarn E 1 x ¾-oz (50-g) ball of Drops Belle Cherry 12

DRESSING THE LOOM: SPEC DETAILS

Sett: 8 ends per inch (2.5 cm)
Warp width: 8½ in. (21.5 cm)
Total warp ends: 68
Beat: 16 picks per inch (2.5 cm)

To dress the loom, wind the warp using the figure-eight method (see page 36). Wind from the top left-hand corner to the right. See overleaf for further instructions on dressing the loom.

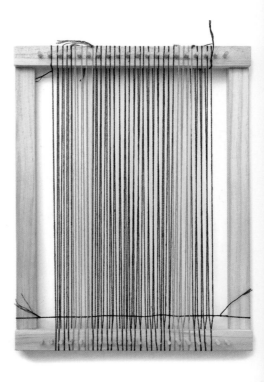

The warp set up for the placemat. The warp is wound in the figure-of-eight method.

Skill level: Moderate

Dimensions: 8¾ x 11¾ in. (22 x 30 cm)

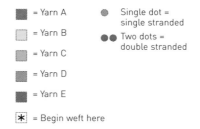

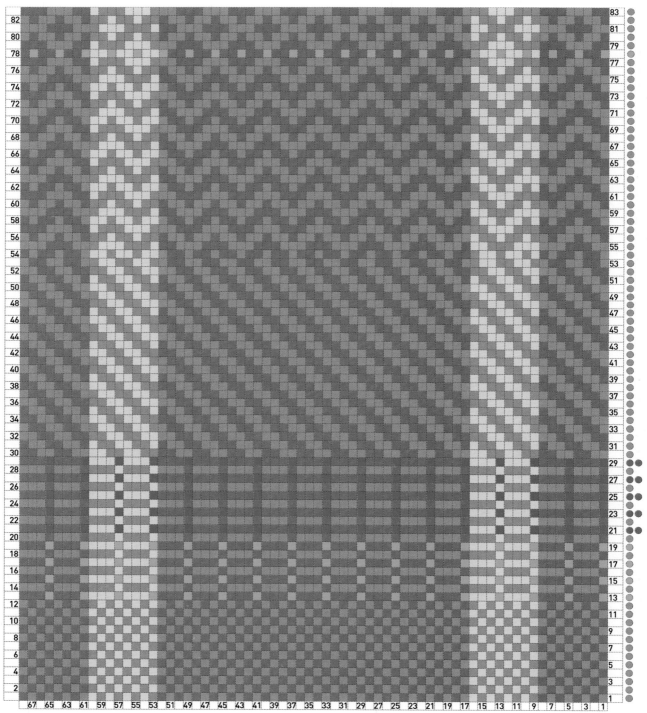

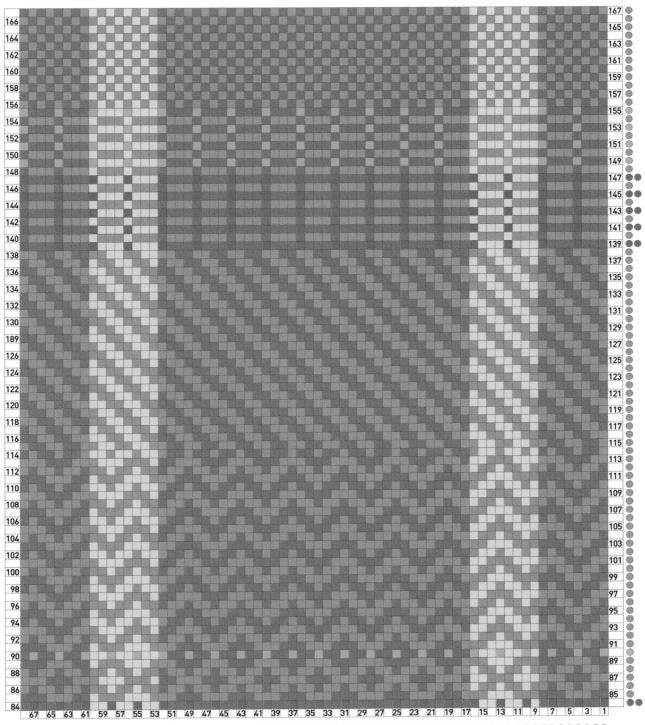

1 To dress the loom, begin at the top left-hand corner of the frame, winding eight threads in Yarn A. Space the warp so that, from the front, there are two threads wound between each wooden peg—this gives an overall sett of eight threads per inch (2.5 cm). Cut Yarn A at the top of the frame and then tie it with Yarn B, so the knot is sitting at the top of the frame. Wind eight threads with Yarn B.

2 After winding eight threads in Yarn B, cut and tie with Yarn A again, then continue to wind a further 36 threads of Yarn A. Again, cut Yarn A and tie with Yarn B, as you did before. Wind Yarn B for eight threads and then join it to Yarn A in order to wind the last eight threads. Finish dressing the loom with a heading cord (see *Setting Up The Frame Loom*, pages 38–40).

3 To begin, weave 12 picks of plain weave (see pages 74–75)—this is approximately ¾ in. (2 cm) of weaving—in Yarn D. This will be used as a rolled-hem edging. Beat firmly, as per the spec details.

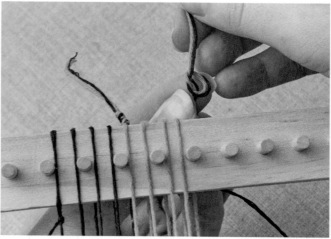

1

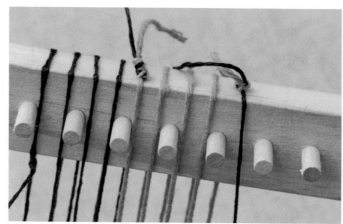

2

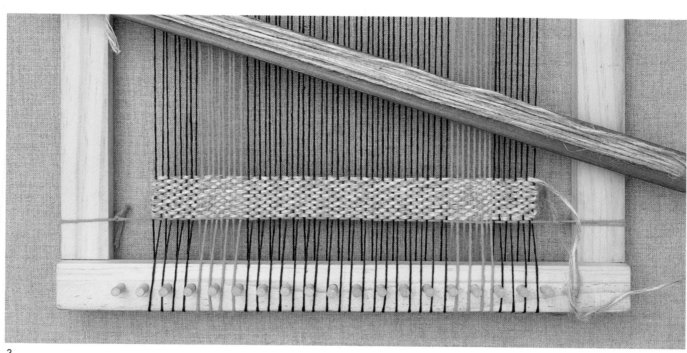

3

4a

4b

5

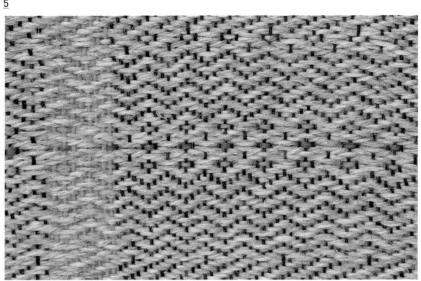

6

4 For the border, following the chart, weave a block of rib (see pages 82–83), alternating between two shuttles, i.e. Shuttle 1 with Yarn D and Shuttle 2 with Yarns C or E, as indicated on the chart (a). Keep both shuttles attached to the weaving and clasp them around each other at the selvages while you weave the rib block (b).

5 Continue following the chart to weave the main body of the placemat in Yarn D. Weave the block of twill (see pages 76–77) for 1½ in. (4 cm) and the block of herringbone weave for 1¼ in. (3 cm). The center of the placemat is woven in traditional bird's eye (see pages 84–85), using Yarn D, with pops of color from Yarns C and E, as indicated. Beat consistently, as before, so that the bird's-eye block measures 1 in. (2.5 cm).

6 After the bird's-eye block, the pattern is then mirrored. Repeat the herringbone, twill, and rib blocks, as before, following the chart. Finish with 12 picks of plain weave (about ¾ in./2 cm of weaving).

Finishing: You can either finish with an edging of hemstitching (see pages 88–89) and trim the warp threads as short fringing or, alternatively, cut the piece from the loom and machine zigzag to edge (see page 87). For this placemat, I finished with a rolled hem. After machine zigzagging, fold over the edges by ½ in. (1 cm) and sew with straight stitch.

CUSHION COVER

———

This handwoven cushion is made from three pieces of cloth: two woolen and one linen-and-cotton mix—a beautiful celebration of natural fibers! It is inspired by my Nordic Lumber Homewares Collection. The pattern follows the traditional bird's eye weave structure, with a slight variation. I love the border panel—which is loosely inspired by Fair Isle gradient knit patterns. Another design idea is to use the cushion cover as a lavender pillow. Simply sew a square cotton cushion insert and fill it with fragrant dried lavender buds!

———

TOOLS

Frame loom with a
12-in. (30-cm) weaving
width
Stick shuttle
Shed stick
Scissors
Beater/fork
Sewing machine
Sewing machine thread
Sewing pins
Iron

Skill level: Moderate

Dimensions: 8 x 8¼ in. (20 x 21 cm)

MATERIALS

Makes 1 cushion cover
1) WOOLEN FRONT CLOTH &
2) WOOLEN REVERSE CLOTH:

Warp:

Yarn A 2 x ¾-oz (50-g) balls of Drops Nepal
Light Gray 0500

Weft:

Yarn B 1 x ¾-oz (50-g) ball of Drops Nepal
Camel 0618

Yarn C 1 x ¾-oz (50-g) ball of Drops Nepal
Medium Brown 0612

Yarn D 1 x ¾-oz (50-g) ball of Drops Alaska
Light Brown 049

Yarn E 1 x ¾-oz (50-g) ball of Drops Nepal
Beige 0300

Yarn F 1 x ¾-oz (50-g) ball of Drops Nepal
Gray 0501

Yarn G 1 x ¾-oz (50-g) ball of Drops Nepal
Light Gray 0500

Yarn H 1 x ¾-oz (50-g) ball of Drops Nepal
Powder Pink 3112

Yarn I 1 x ¾-oz (50-g) ball of Drops Eskimo
Camel 13

3) LINEN-AND-COTTON REVERSE
    CLOTH:

Warp:

Yarn J 1 x ¾-oz (50-g) ball of Drops Bomull-
Lin Brown 05

Weft:

Yarn K 1 x ¾-oz (50-g) ball of Drops Bomull-
Lin Light Beige 03

DRESSING THE LOOM:
SPEC DETAILS

1) WOOLEN FRONT CLOTH &
2) WOOLEN REVERSE CLOTH
Sett: 8 ends per inch (2.5 cm)
Warp width: 12 in. (30 cm)
Total warp ends: 94
Beat: 15 picks per inch (2.5 cm)

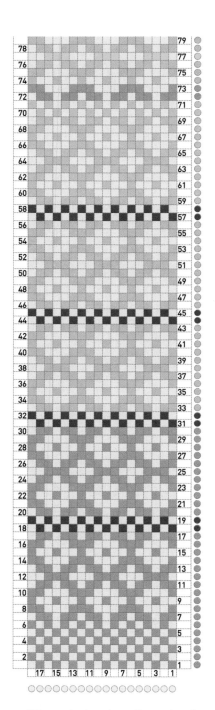

This sample chart shows 18 warp threads—
full size should have 94 warp threads.

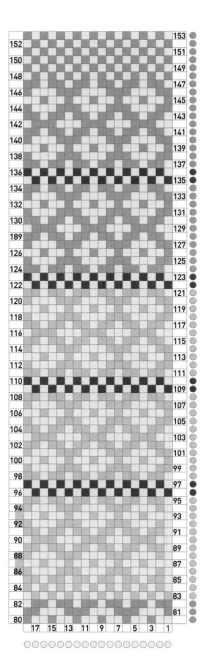

WOOLEN FRONT CLOTH

1 Dress the loom with Yarn A using the figure-eight method (see page 36), as per the spec details on page 116. Finish dressing the loom with a heading cord (see *Setting Up The Frame Loom*, pages 38–40). Following the chart, weave six picks of plain weave (see pages 74–75) in Yarn B. Begin the pattern in Yarn B, as per the chart. Each colored block consists of two repeats of the traditional bird's eye weave structure (see pages 84–85), minus the last pick on the second repeat.

2 Outline each color block with two picks of plain weave in Yarn C. Begin the second block in Yarn D. Remember to keep the beat consistent, at 15 p.p.i. (2.5 cm).

3 Continue weaving as per the chart, building up the gradient of color blocks. Once you have completed the color block in Yarn A, outline with two picks of Yarn G, i.e., picks 73 and 74. This marks the beginning of the center border pattern.

4 The center border follows the same pattern as the color blocks; however, the color changes on each pick. Follow the color changes, as per the chart. Trim and tuck tails on each pick. Once you reach the pick in Yarn H, you have reached the halfway point. The pattern is then mirrored after this—simply repeat the blocks, but in the reverse order, following the chart.

☐	= Yarn A
☐	= Yarn B
☐	= Yarn C
☐	= Yarn D
☐	= Yarn E
☐	= Yarn F
☐	= Yarn G
☐	= Yarn H
☐	= Yarn I
✱	= Begin weft here

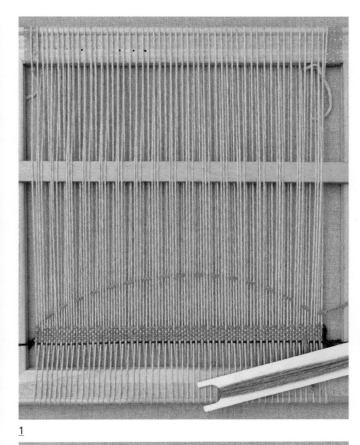

1

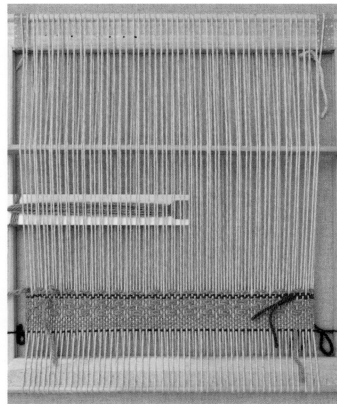

2

3

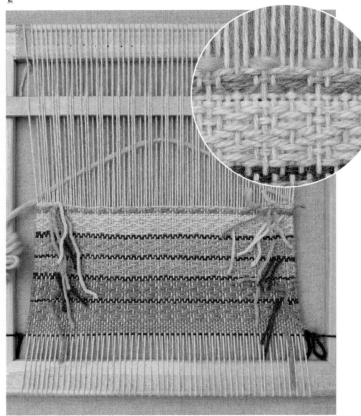

4

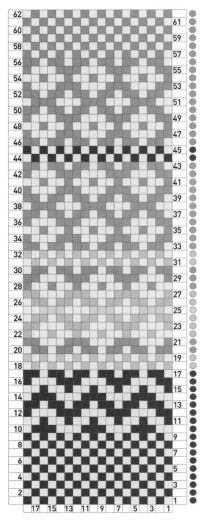

WARP: Yarn A.
Again full size = 94 threads

WOOLEN REVERSE CLOTH

Dress the loom with Yarn A, as per the spec details on page 116, as you did for Woolen Front Cloth. Weave following the chart. This cloth features plain weave (see pages 74–75) and herringbone weave (see pages 78–79) in Yarn C. This is followed by the center border pattern, as woven for the woolen front cloth, and two color blocks in Yarns D and B, all woven in traditional bird's eye. Keep the beat consistent, as per the spec details. The finished woven length on the loom should be approximately 30 in. (12 cm).

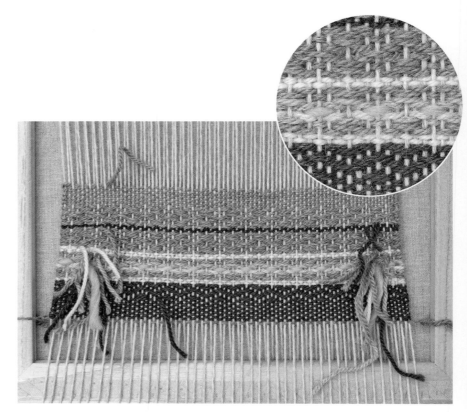

WOOLEN REVERSE CLOTH, FROM THE BACK

☐ = Yarn A

☐ = Yarn B

■ = Yarn C

☐ = Yarn D

☐ = Yarn E

☐ = Yarn F

☐ = Yarn G

☐ = Yarn H

☐ = Yarn I

✱ = Begin weft here

DRESSING THE LOOM: SPEC DETAILS

3) LINEN-AND-COTTON REVERSE CLOTH

Sett: 6 ends per inch (2.5 cm)
Warp width: 12 in. (30 cm)
Total warp ends: 72
Beat: 22 picks per inch (2.5 cm)

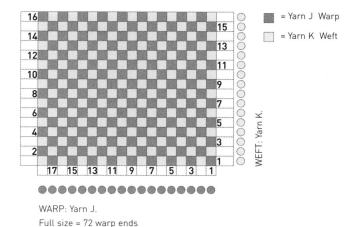

■ = Yarn J Warp
□ = Yarn K Weft

WEFT: Yarn K.

WARP: Yarn J.
Full size = 72 warp ends

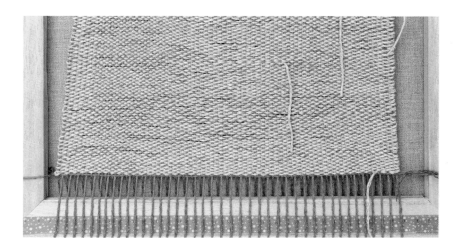

PLAIN-WEAVE REVERSE CLOTH ON THE LOOM

LINEN-AND-COTTON REVERSE CLOTH

The reverse cloth is a simple cloth woven entirely in plain weave with a single weft. Dress the loom with Yarn I, using the figure-eight method (see page 36), as per the spec details listed left. Weave in plain weave with Yarn J. Be careful to beat the weft firmly and keep the beat consistent. Aim for 22 picks per inch (2.5 cm). Weave to a total length of 8¾ in. (22 cm) on the loom. To take all three pieces off the loom, cut and machine zigzag to edge (see page 87).

To finish all the cloths, follow the wet finishing techniques on pages 98–99. Ensure you wash the linen-and-cotton cloth separately to the woolens, because they will need different washing temperatures.

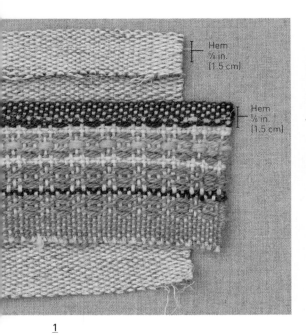

1

2

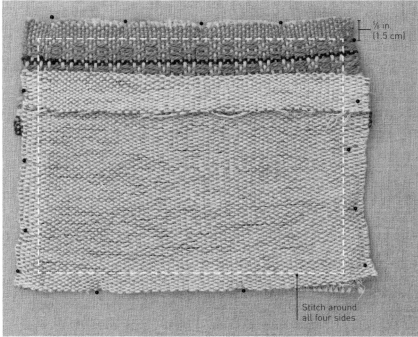

3

CUSHION COVER CONSTRUCTION

1 The cushion is constructed with an envelope back, meaning there is no need for a zipper fastening. First, hem both of the reverse cloths by ⅝ in. (1.5 cm), as shown above. On the reverse woolen cloth, hem the herringbone patterned edge. Trim any loose threads.

2 To construct the cover, place the front cloth on a work surface, facing up. Lay the woolen reverse cloth on top, so the two pieces are face to face. Place the reverse linen-and-cotton cloth on top, again face down. Ensure both hemmed edges of the reverse cloths overlap in the middle by approximately 15 in. (6 cm) and that all other edges are lined up. Pin in place.

3 Using a straight stitch setting on your sewing machine, stitch all four sides of the cover, taking a ⅝-in. (1.5-cm) seam allowance. Trim any loose threads. Press the seam and turn the cover the right side out using the "envelope" opening. (If you would like to make a lavender cushion insert, see overleaf.)

1

2

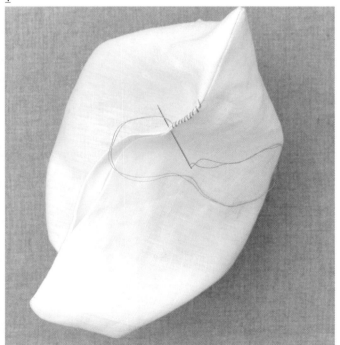

3

LAVENDER CUSHION INSERT

You can sew a simple insert filled with dried lavender buds if you want to use your cushion as a relaxing lavender pillow.

1 Use a piece of cotton fabric measuring approximately 11 x 18 in. (28 x 45 cm). Fold the fabric in half, right sides together, and pin in place. With your sewing machine, sew along the three sides, taking a ⅝-in. (1.5-cm) seam allowance. Leave one-third of the side opposite the fold unsewn, to act as an opening.

2 Press the seams and trim any loose threads. Turn the insert right side out out through the unsewn opening. Press. Fill two-thirds of the insert with dried lavender buds.

3 To complete the insert, handsew the opening with a needle and thread. Push the insert inside the cushion cover—and enjoy the fragrance!

LOOPED BAG

———

This bag project involves double-sided weaving—that is, weaving on both sides of the frame loom. The technique creates an exciting woven tubular structure. You will be "weaving in the round"—to steal a phrase from knitting. The structure is inspired by a piece I wove on a cardboard loom when I was in primary school. The design features a looped pattern that is inspired by the recent trend for "carpet tote" bags.

———

TOOLS

Basic frame loom measuring 16 x 16 in. (40 x 40 cm)

Masking tape

2 rods

2 stick shuttles

Scissors

Beater/fork

Naalbinding needle

28½ x 16½-in. (72 x 42-cm) piece of lightweight cotton lining fabric

Sewing needle and thread

MATERIALS

Makes 1 looped bag

Warp:

Yarn A 2 x ¾-oz (50-g) balls of Drops Nepal Light Gray 0500

Weft:

Yarn B 2 x 3½-oz (100-g) balls of Drops Andes Red 3946

Yarn C 1 x ¾-oz (50-g) ball of Drops Alaska Light Brown 49

DRESSING THE LOOM: SPEC DETAILS

Sett: 5 ends per ¾ in. (2 cm)
Warp width: 15¾ in. (40 cm) per side
Total warp ends: 100 per side
Beat: 8 p.p.i. in Yarn B; 10 p.p.i. for the Looped pattern section. 10 picks per inch (2.5 cm)

The bag is woven on both sides of the loom— the warp is dressed in a circular motion around the front and reverse of the loom using one continuous warp yarn.

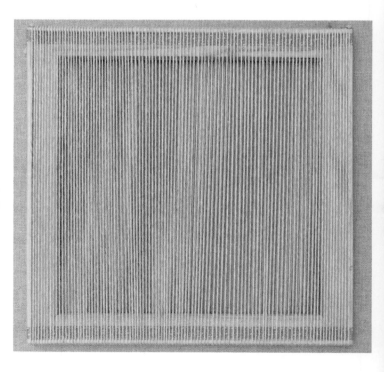

Skill level: Moderate

Dimensions: 11 x 15 in. (28 x 39 cm)

1

2

3

1 To dress the loom for a double-sided weave, the warp is dressed in a circular motion around the front and reverse of the loom using one continuous warp yarn. Tape the end of the warp yarn, Yarn A, securely to the top left-hand corner of the frame, as shown.

2 Bring the warp yarn down to the base of the frame loom, holding it under an even tension as you do so.

3 Turn the frame over and wind the warp yarn back up to the top of the frame. Continue winding the warp from top to base at the front, then turning the frame over and winding from base to top on the reverse, setting the warp at five ends per ¾ in. (2 cm). Make sure to keep the tension even across the warp.

4 Keep winding in this way until you reach the right-hand corner of the frame and have a total of 100 warp threads per side. Cut the warp yarn and tape the end securely to the top right-hand corner of the frame.

☐ = Yarn A

▨ = Yarn C

▧ = Yarn B

✳ = Begin weft here

◊ = Loop

5 Begin weaving on the right-hand side on the front with a shuttle of Yarn B. Weave one pick of plain weave (see pages 74–75) on the front, from right to left. Beat the weft so that it lies as close to the frame edge as possible. Beat hard!

6 Turn the loom over. With the same weft and shuttle, weave one pick of plain weave from right to left. Beat firmly as before, so that the weft lies snug to the frame edge. You have now completed one rotation of weaving in the round!

7 Continue weaving in the round with Yarn B, beating firmly so that all the picks are sitting close to each other. Weave for eight picks (i.e. eight rotations), until the section of weaving is approximately 1 in. (2.5 cm) in height.

8 Leaving Yarn B attached to the shuttle, begin weaving on the front side with a second shuttle of Yarn C. This second shuttle with Yarn C will weave the ground weft of the looped pattern. Weave one rotation of plain weave from right to left. Alternate between Yarn B and C for the next two rotations, as per the chart.

9 On the next round of Yarn B, the looping pattern begins. Weave Yarn B as plain weave. Following the chart, use a rod to pick up and wrap the weft floats to form the start of the looped pattern (see *Looping*, pages 70–71). Leave the rod in place. Turn the loom over and repeat on the reverse side. Turn the loom to the front again and gently remove the first rod. Weave one pick of Yarn C. Beat firmly. Turn the loom over and repeat on the reverse.

10 Continue weaving in the round, alternating between Yarn B for every looped pick and Yarn C for every ground-weft pick. Increase or decrease the loops gradually, as per the chart, to create the triangles and diamonds.

11 Once the chart is complete, cut and tuck in Yarn C. Weave 14 rotations of Yarn B—this will be approximately 2 in. (5 cm) (a). To finish, weave Yarn B in the round for approximately 4 in. (10 cm), and cut and tuck the tail (b).

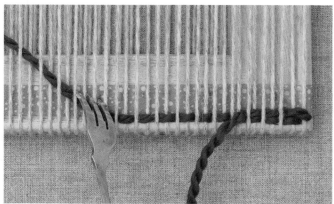

5

6

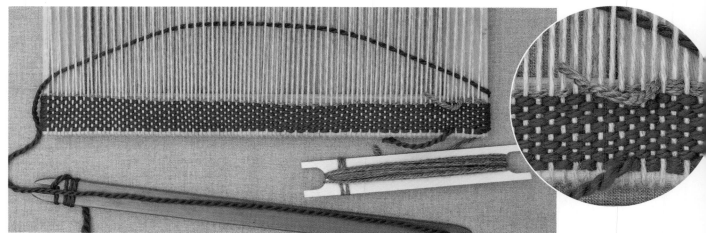

7–8

9

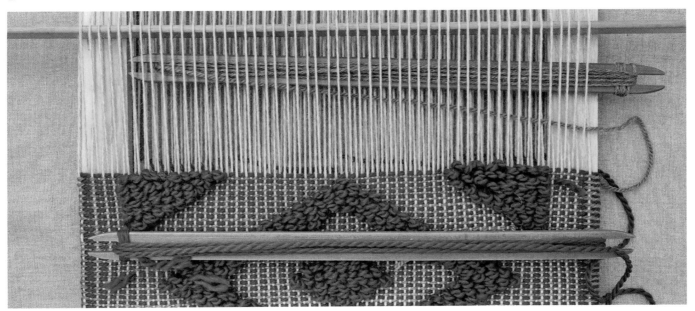

10

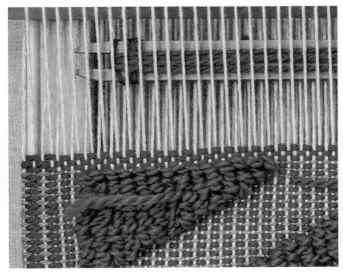

11a

11b

12 Cut three strands of yarn B, approximately 47 in. (120 cm) in length. Using the naalbinding needle, weave three picks of plain weave on all three sides of the bag. With the first strand, begin at the top right-hand side, with the needle traveling over one, under one (a). Continue in this way across the base of the frame and then up the left-hand side of the frame. Beat close to the frame edge. Leave the ends loose. Repeat for the second and third strands (b). Weave an extra two picks across the base to give a total of five picks (c). Tuck the tails.

13 To remove the weaving from the loom, carefully cut all the warp threads across the top of the frame.

14 Gently slide the weaving downward on the frame and pull it off!

15 The looped bag has been woven in a tubular form. There should now be no gaps visible on the selvages.

16 Machine zigzag the edging (see page 87) and trim the warp threads.

<u>12a</u>

<u>12b</u>

<u>12c</u>

13

14

15

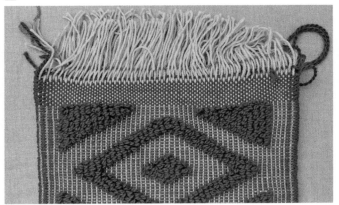

16

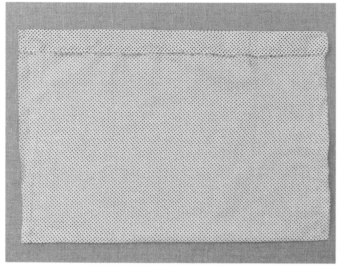

1

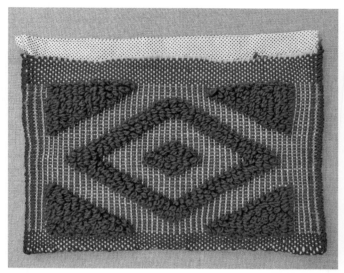

2

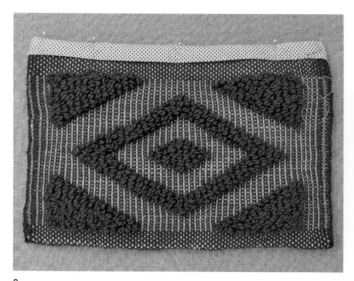

3

4

BAG CONSTRUCTION

1 To line the bag, edge the short sides of the lining fabric with a 1-in. (2.5-cm) hem. Fold the hemmed lining fabric in half, with the right sides facing. Pin and sew the unhemmed two sides (seam allowance ⅝ in./1.5 cm). Press the seams open and trim any loose threads.

2 Insert the lining bag into the woven bag, wrong sides facing.

3 For the outer hem, fold down the hemmed edge of the lining by 1 in. (2.5 cm), and pin.

4 Handstitch the cotton lining to the woven bag.

To finish the bag, sew on some leather handles.

TIP After lining the bag, you could also add a zipper to the opening. The bag could then be used as a perfectly padded laptop case.

GLOSSARY

——

BALANCED WEAVE
When there are the same number of warp ends per unit of measurement as there are weft picks over the same unit of measurement.

BAST
From plant stems (see *Meet the Materials*, pages 22–27).

BEAT
The confirming of a pick into position using a beater. As a noun, it means the number of picks per unit of measurement.

BEATER
The implement used to beat down each weft shot after weaving (see *How to Hand Weave*). A weaving comb or a kitchen fork can be used for this task in frame loom weaving.

BLOCK
One pattern or threading unit, or one area forming a separate section. As a verb, it means to set a piece of work into shape.

BOBBIN (TAPESTRY)
Small spool wound with weft yarn, used as a shuttle.

BODKIN
A needle with a blunt end.

BOLL
Seedpod of the cotton plant.

CONE
Yarn wound onto a conical shape.

COUNT
The thickness of the yarn.

DENT
The space between two pegs or slits across the top and base bar of a frame loom.

DRAFT
The diagrammatic representation of the threading order, the weaving sequence and, by these, the cloth structure.

DRESSING THE LOOM
Placing the warp onto the loom—winding, tensioning, and tying.

END
A warp thread.

FABRIC
Cloth, textile, or a woven piece.

FACE OF CLOTH
The top side of the fabric. Weaving may be done face down so that the face is on the underside of the weaving.

FELL
The position during weaving after the last pick.

FIBER
The small hairlike units that are spun into yarn. May be natural or man-made.

FILAMENT
A continuous length of fiber such as silk or man-made.

FINISHING
The work done to the woven piece after it has been removed from the loom.

FRINGE
The ends of the warp either left loose or grouped. Can also be made with Rya Knots (See *Rug-making Techniques*, pages 64–85 and *Edging Techniques*, pages 86–99).

FULLING
A finishing technique—working the wet woven piece so that the structure melds together.

GROUND CLOTH
The basic interlaced structure of a patterned cloth.

INTERLACE
The interweaving of warp and weft.

INTERSECT
The movement from front to back and back to front of a warp end or weft pick.

LOOM WASTE
That portion of the warp that cannot be woven (generally one-third on a frame loom).

MENDING
Darning in loose threads and broken ends, and replacing wrong picks prior to wet finishing.

PICK (SHOT)
A single inserted row of weft yarn.

PLAIN WEAVE (ALSO CALLED TABBY)
The warp and weft interlace by moving over and under single threads.

PLY
The twisting together of two or more single strands of yarn.

SELVAGE
The closed woven edge on either side of the cloth.

SETT
The number of ends per measuring unit. Also the number of picks per unit.

SETTING UP
See *Setting up the Frame Loom*, pages 36–41.

SHED
The name given to the triangular space or opening between two sets of warp threads—those that are raised and those that are lowered—into which the weft is placed.

• Natural shed—Have a look just under the top bar of your dressed loom. The two sets of warp threads are separated by the depth of the frame. This is the natural shed.
• Alternate shed—The "alternate shed" is made when the lower warp threads are raised to the front and the raised warp threads are pushed to the back.

SHOT
See Pick.

SHUTTLE
The stick or implement that holds the weft.

SINGLES
Fibers spun or twisted into a single strand.

SPOOL
Yarn on a small tube.

STAPLE
The length of the individual fiber.

STICKS
• Shed—Thin broad stick inserted into the warp that can be turned on edge to provide a shed.
• Tension—A stick, inserted under some of the warp ends behind the top bar of the frame loom while dressing the loom under, removed to loosen tension on warp threads when too taut.

SKEIN
A length of yarn, loosely coiled and knotted (see *How to Wind A Finger Skein*, page 45).

TAKE-UP
The reduction in length of the warp and width of the weft due to interlacement.

TASSEL
A bound bunch of threads.

TEETH (PEGS)
The dividers in the top and base bar of the frame loom, usually pegs or slits.

TENSION
The degree to which the warp is stretched during weaving. Also, the degree to which the weft is stretched.

THREAD
A long, thin strand of any type of fiber used in sewing or weaving.

THRUMS
The waste ends of the warp that cannot be woven.

TWILL
Weaving a set combination of adjacent ends together by sequential raising or lowering of those sets. (See *Weave Structures*, pages 72–85.)

TWIST
The spin given to a yarn to give it strength.

WARP
The threads stretching vertically from the top bar to the base bar of the loom. Also the threads along the length of the cloth.

WARP-FACED
Weaving in which the warp threads are dominant on the surface.

WARPING
See *Setting up the Frame Loom*, pages 36–41.

WEAVE
The systematic order of interlacements of warp and weft threads.

WEB
An older term for the cloth on the loom.

WEFT
The yarn passing from side to side. Also the yarns along the width of the cloth.

WEFT-FACED
Weaving in which the weft threads are dominant on the surface.

YARN
Fibers spun into thread-like form. Also, the type of thread used.

INDEX

—

CREDITS

———

I WOULD LIKE TO THANK:

Quarto, for giving me the opportunity to create *Weaving on a Little Loom*—
a journey I have found thoroughly rewarding and one I am truly thankful
for. The fantastic team there made the writing of this book so enjoyable and
I would like to thank them for all of their tremendous hard work; turning my
words, tutorials, and designs into a beautiful, succinct book—Kate Burkett,
Kate Kirby, Jackie Palmer, Moira Clinch, Caroline Guest, Lily de Gatacre,
and Samantha Warrington.

Photographers Phil Wilkins and Nicki Dowey, for the entertaining shoot
days and stunning photography, and illustrator Kuo Kang Chen, for
designing beautiful charts to communicate my project designs.

Mary and John Daly, for all of your support as always and especially to
Mary for the beautiful portrait shot on page 9.

Damien, without whom there would be no book. Thank you for your endless
encouragement, enthusiasm, and motivation, especially during the writing
of this book, throughout which your home has been overflowing with yarn,
frame looms, and charts.

The many, many weavers and makers I have met so far on my weaving
journey who have inspired me—thank you all!

Quarto would also like to thank The Handweavers Studio & Gallery,
in particular Dawn and Taslima, for their help sourcing yarns and
weaving up swatches.

the handweavers studio

Fiona Daly and Quarto would also like to thank Drops Yarn for providing
the majority of yarns used in this book (see www.garnstudio.com).

DROPS Design®